THOMAS J. "STONEWALL"
JACKSON

Great American Generals
THOMAS J. "STONEWALL" JACKSON

Bronwyn Mills

GALLERY BOOKS
An imprint of W.H. Smith Publishers Inc.
112 Madison Avenue
New York, New York 10016

Published by Gallery Books
A Division of W H Smith Publishers Inc.
112 Madison Avenue
New York, New York 10016

Produced by
Brompton Books Corp.
15 Sherwood Place
Greenwich, CT 06830

ISBN 0-8317-4078-7

Printed in Hong Kong

10 9 8 7 6 5 4 3 2 1

Page 1: *An encamped battery of the Confederate Army.*

Page 2: *Scenes from three of Stonewall Jackson's most famous battles. From top to bottom: Antietam, 1862; Fredericksburg, 1862; and Chancellorsville, 1863.*

Page 3: *A detail taken from an old engraving of Jackson at Chancellorsville. He is already being portrayed as a larger-than-life hero.*

Pages 4-5: *The Confederate fortifications at Fredericksburg.*

PICTURE CREDITS

Brompton Photo Library: 21(left), 25, 41(bottom), 47(top), 50(top), 59(both).
Anne S.K. Brown Military Collection, Brown University; 15 (bottom), 18-19, 22-23(both), 24(both), 30-31(center), 35, 47(bottom), 59(top), 62-63(top), 68-69, 70(both), 74(bottom), 78(top).
Chicago Historical Society: 42-43, 46, 56-57.
Rutherford B. Hayes Presidential Center: 19(right), 30(left), 31(right), 36(left), 45, 60, 61(top).
Library of Congress: 6-7(both), 8-9, 10-11, 12(left), 14, 16(top), 17, 20, 21(right), 28, 32, 33, 34(bottom), 38(top), 44(both), 49 (bottom), 51(both), 52, 53(top), 54-55(all three), 59(bottom right), 62(bottom), 64, 66-67, 72, 74(top), 75, 76-77, 78(bottom), 79.
National Archives: 11(right), 12-13, 18(left), 26-27, 36-37, 53 (bottom), 56(bottom left), 58-59(bottom), 65, 73(both).
Richard Natkiel: 15(top), 34(top), 39, 71.
Peter Newark's Western Americana: 38(bottom).
New York Public Library, Picture Collection: 41(top), 63(bottom), 68(left).
Norfolk Southern Corporation: 48-49(top), 50(bottom).
U.S. Army Photograph: 29.
Virginia State Library: 16(bottom), 40, 56(top left).
V M I Museum: 61(bottom).

ACKNOWLEDGMENTS
The publisher would like to thank the following people who helped in the preparation of this book: Don Longabucco, who designed it; Rita Longabucco, who did the picture research; and John Kirk, who edited the text.

Contents

Early Years

One of the anecdotes that Lt. Col. William W. Blackford, Confederate calvary staff, told of Stonewall Jackson, concerned the Battle of Malvern Hill. Apparently on July 1, 1862, Jackson, who was the Confederate commander, turned to a most peculiar task: he ordered that all the Confederate soldiers who had fallen that day be stacked neatly in rows, with blankets and oilcloths spread over their bodies and covering their faces. Then General Jackson had his men go back and tidy up the field of battle itself. When Blackford asked his general why he was doing this, Old Stonewall replied, "Well, I am going to attack here presently, as soon as the fog rises, and it won't do to march the troops over their own dead, you know."

The anecdote is illustrative because it speaks to a point that many people raised about Jackson during his lifetime and have raised ever since: that the man was decidedly eccentric. Well, perhaps. But if his behavior often was unorthodox, that is not necessarily the same as saying that it was ill-considered. For whatever he did, Jackson usually had a good – though not always obvious – reason.

The name Stonewall Jackson to this day conjures up a memory of heroism in both North and South, and had Jackson not died early in the War Between the States, the course of that conflict might have been quite different. For what-

Left: *A cotton plantation on the Mississippi. A highly profitable, labor-intensive crop, cotton depended on the institution of slavery for its ascendancy to its position as the major cash crop in the Deep South prior to the Civil War.*

Left: *In a picture rendered 44 years after his death, General Stonewall Jackson is depicted with his early boyhood home, situated on the West Fork River in Lewis County, Virginia (now West Virginia).*

Overleaf: *On May 14, 1862, a group of contrabands, slaves taken behind Federal lines, were photographed on a farm in Virginia. On this day General Jackson was moving against Union forces in the Shenandoah Valley Campaign.*

ever might be said of his personal peculiarities, no one has ever doubted that Stonewall Jackson was one of the most brilliant military strategists this country has ever produced.

Jackson was born January 21, 1824, in Clarksburg, Harrison County, Virginia (now West Virginia), the third of four children born to Julia Neale Jackson and Johnathan Jackson. A charming but spendthrift lawyer, Johnathan Jackson belonged to a prominent family from Weston, Virginia. Like their Irish ancestors before them, the entire Jackson clan was composed of country squires, and together they owned more property and slaves, held more public offices and lived in better homes than any of their western Virginia neighbors. Julia Neale, however, resisted their influence and named her son not after a Jackson, but after her father, Thomas. Only when nearly grown did Jackson add the middle name of Johnathan, after his father.

Johnathan Jackson never did accumulate many assets, and the patriarch of the Jackson clan, Uncle Cummins Jackson, was more than once called upon to bail out his nephew when Johnathan's charms failed to rescue him from bad investments and gambling debts. Unfortunately, even after he married Julia Neale his vices persisted. In 1827 Johnathan's oldest daughter, Elizabeth, contracted typhoid, and, in spite of her father's personal care, she died. Shortly thereafter Johnathan himself caught the dreaded disease and also died. Now his habitual lack of thrift came home with a vengeance: his young widow and three remaining children were left destitute and had to sell their home.

Because his father's reputation was already tarnished and because he had left them in such dire straits, young Thomas soon heard unpleasant talk of his father. Certainly his father's shame was a source of distress to Jackson for many years after. Thomas saw his mother struggle: she was outwardly cheerful and entertaining in social situations, but she was often quite depressed at home. Indeed, although

the fact is not much publicized, she came close to having the nineteenth-century version of a nervous breakdown.

The clan and the community did what it could. The local Masonic Lodge gave the widow a small house, and Julia Neale taught school and took in sewing to help make ends meet. But when Julia Neale remarried, to a Captain Blake B. Woodson, it became difficult to live under the shadow of the Jackson family, and the couple moved farther west. Julia's health was delicate, however, and Thomas and his sister Laura were soon sent back to live with Uncle Cummins

Jackson at Jackson's Mill in Weston. Warren, the eldest child, was sent to live with his Uncle, Alfred Neale.

Julia's illness worsened, and once more the three young children traveled to their mother's side. Close to death, she blessed them and admonished them to live "by the laws of God, as revealed in the Bible." She died in September, 1831, of complications of childbirth. Wrote Woodson to his grieving stepson: "Death with her had no sting. The grave could claim no victory. I have known of few women of equal, none of superior merit. She was buried the day before yesterday

Left: *After he was orphaned at the age of seven, Jackson spent the remaining years of his childhood at Jackson's Mill, his Uncle Cummin's small estate in Weston.*

Above: *The mill at Jackson's Mill. The self-sufficient estate provided everything but good schooling, and young Jackson was academically unprepared for West Point.*

with all the solemnity due to such a person and on such an occasion."

To Thomas, however, these words were hollow: he never quite forgave his stepfather for taking Julia Neale's body to the hills, burying it in an overgrown graveyard and in an unmarked grave. Many times Jackson rode back to the mountain village of Ansted where his mother died, looking through that derelict cemetery for her grave; but he found none that he could identify with certainty. It was not until after he died that one of his brigade marked what he deter-

mined as the grave with an inscription: "To the mother of Stonewall Jackson, This tribute from one of his old brigade."

Thus Thomas was orphaned at seven years of age. From the day of his mother's death onward, admiring biographers are fond of writing, he began and ended each day in prayer, though it was many years before he joined any organized denomination.

Jackson spent the remaining years of his childhood at Jackson's Mill. Like Mount Vernon, but considerably less elegant, the estate was a self-sufficient village worked by the owners and a few slaves. It contained a sawmill, stables, workshops, grinding machinery, fertile land and a large log-cabin-style manor house. Uncle Cummins and his young nephew grew quite close. The uncle regularly brought the young boy along with him to house raisings, corn huskings and other events where there was dancing and drinking and cards, though Jackson was more an observer than a participant. He never would become a carouser; he later explained that he liked "spiritous liquors," but found them too strong and so gave them up early.

Though life at Jackson's Mill appeared to be an idyllic place for two orphans, it was also a worldly, increasingly masculine environment. In August, 1835, Thomas' much-loved step-grandmother died, and the last of his two maiden aunts, Aunt Peggy, married and moved away. It was then decided, that Laura should be best off living with her mother's family; and at eleven, Jackson saw his sister ride away behind the saddle of another aunt, Rebecca Jackson White, en route to the Neales in Ohio.

Thomas was then briefly sent to stay with his Uncle

Brake, who lived a few miles from Clarksburg. Within, however, a day or two, Jackson returned, explaining to a cousin in his typical taciturn way, "Uncle Brake and I don't agree; I have quit him, and shall not go back any more." His bachelor uncles, who loved him, did not protest.

Uncle Cummins was an energetic man whom one chronicler described as "utterly devoid of Christianity." Several inches above six feet, he stooped whenever he had to enter a door. He was quick-minded, though perhaps a kingmaker rather than a king, and it was a surprise to many that Tom didn't grow to be a replica of his charistmatic uncle.

Jackson's Mill had one serious shortcoming, and that was that it lacked good schooling. Children there had sporadic classes whenever a teacher could be found, and young Tom educated himself mostly through his own efforts and his Bible reading. Despite this, Thomas Jackson was awarded the post of Constable to the Lewis County Courthouse. Family influence had been exerted upon the Justice of the Peace in charge, Col. Alexander Scott Withers – necessarily, since Tom was both technically too young for the post and another candidate had received more votes for the position than he.

The intrigues which gained young Thomas an appointment to West Point were even more complicated. Jackson was the community's second choice for nomination. But after going to see West Point, the chosen candidate, Gibson Butcher, decided that he simply did not like it there. Then Uncle Cummins Jackson got Butcher to write a letter of resignation to West Point, to be hand-carried by Thomas Jackson, ". . . also an applicant for the appointment." With this and four thick letters praising him as a candidate, Jackson set off to see his Congressman, Representative Hays, and then the Secretary of War, J. C. Spencer, and to persuade them to accept "Thomas J. Jackson," as he now called himself. By the time he reached the Secretary of War, this strategy had won him the appointment. Thus on July 1, 1842, Jackson was enrolled at West Point.

Imagine Jackson, in homespun, heavy riding boots and

Below: *First Lieutenant of Artillery Stonewall Jackson, from a photograph taken on August 20, 1847, during the Mexican War. He had been promoted for gallantry at Vera Cruz.*

Right: *A view of old West Point, attended by Jackson from 1842 to 1846. Though unprepared at first, he worked hard as a cadet and was graduated 17th in a distinguished class.*

broad-brimmed hat, getting off the train and trudging the last few miles to the Academy with heavy gear and grimy saddlebags. Observing his arrival, two of his future Confederate colleagues, J. E. B. Stuart and James Longstreet exchanged remarks.

"Who is that gawk?" queried Cadet Stuart.

"I don't know," answered Longstreet, "but I'll bet my bottom dollar that gawk will make good here."

Academically behind, Jackson found West Point at first difficult. On January 28, 1844, he wrote to his sister, Laura: "I am almost homesick, and expect to continue so until I can have a view of my native mountains, and receive the greetings of my friends and relatives . . . ." Jackson went on to describe his aspirations. He wrote that if he was graduated

in the top half of his class, he would be paid $1000 a year; in the lower half (as an infantryman), $750 a year, "But I feel very confident that . . . I shall graduate in the upper half of my class, and high enough to enter the Dragoons." Yet Jackson still did not then see himself as a career army man: "I intend to remain in the army no longer than I can get rid of it with honor, and mean to commence some professional business at home."

By May of 1845, however, Jackson's confidence had grown. In another letter to Laura he noted that his academic standing had improved and that he had begun to consider a military career after all: "I have before me two courses, either of which I may choose. The first would be to follow the profession of arms. . . ."

A Time for War, a Time for Peace

In April, 1846, just a few months before his graduation from West Point, Jackson penned the famous understatement, "Rumor appears to indicate a rupture between our government and the Mexican." On June 30, as General Zachary Taylor and his army were about to cross the Rio Grande and invade Matamoros, Thomas J. Jackson left the Academy, graduated 17th in his class, with a commission as Brevet Second Lieutenant of Artillery. After a brief visit home, in July he received orders to join Company K of the First Regiment of the Artillery and to proceed with the troops to Point Isabel, Texas. He was then 22 years of age.

The Mexican War was not to be solely Jackson's first taste of battle. It also hastened the beginning of the Civil War, for the annexation of Texas – which precipitated the Mexican war – added a vast tract of pro-slavery territory to the US. Moreover, in the battles in Mexico the young Jackson was to encounter many of the same people who would fight in the Civil War, and much of his thinking about military strategy began to take shape at this time.

The landing of US troops under General Winfield Scott at Vera Cruz on March 9, 1847. As a brevet second lieutenant, First United States Artillery, Jackson went to Mexico to fight under General Zachary Taylor. Transferred to Scott's army, Jackson served with distinction at Vera Cruz.

The Mexican War, seen in retrospect, was one of the most unpopular wars in United States history, but Jackson, as a military man, never questioned it. He had little capacity for generalized thought and lacked the inquiring mind of his predecessor at the Academy, Robert E. Lee. Jackson was a man of action and duty, who prided himself on respect for authority and "doing the right thing," and he was unabashedly gung-ho. He wrote to his sister on March 30, 1847: "I have been at Matamoras, Camargo, Monterrey and Saltillo and the intermediate towns. . . . It would have afforded me much pleasure to have been with the gallant and victorious General Taylor at the Battle of Buena Vista, in which he has acquired laurels as imperishable as the history which shall record the invasion of Mexico by our victorious armies."

Jackson's first major experience of action began on March 9 when US forces under General Winfield Scott invaded Mexico from the sea at Vera Cruz. Huge navy guns shelled the besieged city, and Jackson directed a unit that did the short-range shooting. On March 29 the city at last fell, and US forces (with only 64 men dead and wounded) captured both the 4000-man garrison and 400 cannon. But for the use of artillery the fall of Vera Cruz might not have been accomplished, and officers observing Jackson's conduct as he helped direct some of this firepower were well aware of his contribution. Within a month Jackson was promoted from a second lieutenant to a first lieutenant for "gal-

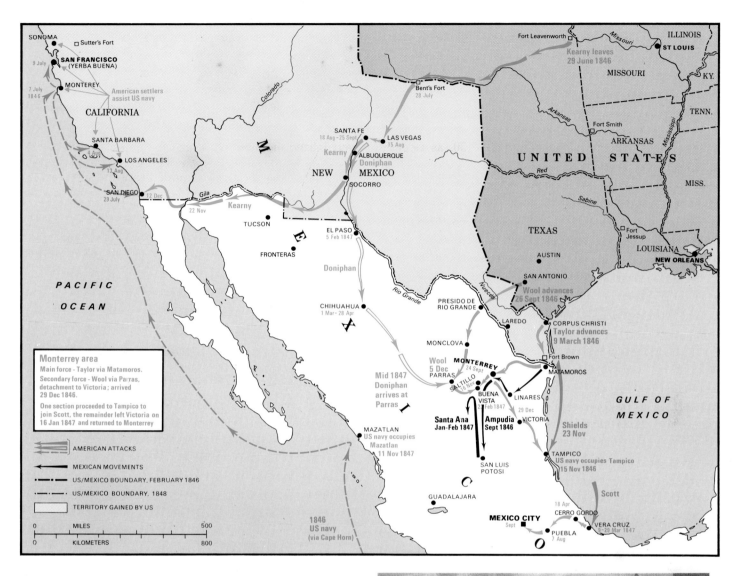

Above: *Map of American troop movements in the Mexican War.*

Right: *Portrait of General Zachary Taylor at the time of his command in Mexico.*

lant and meritorious conduct at the siege of Vera Cruz."

From Vera Cruz, Scott intended to march his army to Mexico City, 200 miles to the west, but between Vera Cruz and the plateau on which Mexico City was situated was a jungle-choked plain and narrow roads leading through mountain passes. The first of these passes was at Cerro Gordo. There the Mexicans, superior in numbers and matériel, made a stand, but on April 16, 1847, the US troops scored an astonishing victory. Though Jackson did not participate in the attack, he helped pursue the enemy as far as Puebla, 80 miles east of Mexico City. Puebla fell without resistance.

Losses from illness and battle casualties had by now reduced US numbers by half, and Scott was obliged to do a good deal of ad hoc reorganizing. Jackson was transferred to Company G and ordered to garrison the town of Jalapa, northeast of Puebla. Disappointed, he wrote hime, "I have

STORMING OF THE CASTLE OF CHAPULTEPEC, BY THE AMERICAN ARMY UNDER GENERAL SCOTT, SEPT. 13, 1847.

Left: *General Winfield Scott, nicknamed "Old Fuss and Feathers" for his stern formality, took Mexico City September 14, 1847. Later he became the first to hold the rank of lieutenant general since George Washington.*

Above: *Troops under General Winfield Scott storm the castle of Chapultepec on the route to Mexico City. This depiction of the historic battle appeared July 4, 1848, in the* Pictorial Brother Jonathan.

the mortification to be left behind," and he speculated that God Himself might have meant to diminish "my excessive ambition."

During this relatively peaceful interlude, during which he acquired an appreciation of Spanish ladies and a fondness for fresh fruit, Jackson tried to analyze what he had so far learned about military strategy. First, he concluded that tying an army up in a siege, as the army had done at Vera Cruz, should be avoided if at all possible. It gained nothing – as Jackson would later observe of the Confederates at Richmond – but casualties.

Second, he decided that it was always better to attack than to mark time or defend, even when the enemy had superior numbers. This lesson Jackson credited to the examples of both Zachery Taylor and Scott.

Third, he criticized Taylor for not immediately following up his major victory at Buena Vista and laying waste to the retreating enemy, a tactic that would later become a Jackson signature. But he nevertheless greatly approved of the way Taylor personally moved about on the battlefield so that he could see for himself what was going on. And he also admired Taylor's refusal to kowtow to military orthodoxy.

Another officer whom Jackson admired was Captain John Bankhead Magruder, who used "flying artillery" to storm the opposing troops; that is, he mounted light cannons on horseback and raced them into the thick of the battle, sometimes spending blood as if it were inexhaustible. This, too, fit into Jackson's notions of warfare, and he agitated mightily to be taken out of Jalapa and sent back into battle under Magruder.

When Jackson finally got his way he galloped southeast towards Puebla, where, after months of delay, Scott was preparing to leave for Mexico City. It was August 7 when Scott marched from the garrison at Puebla with four divisions. Among them were Jackson's old outfit, Company K, under General David Twiggs, and General Gideon Pillow's division, to which Magruder was assigned and to which Jackson now reported. At the rear of the assembled troops were scouts and engineers, including Captain Robert E. Lee and Pierre Gustave Toutant Beauregard, another future Confederate officer.

On August 10 the US troops crossed the Rio Frio Mountains, 10,000 feet above sea level. Descending, they saw the full sweep of the valley of Mexico and, as Scott so imperiously put it, "that splendid city [which] shall soon be ours!" But between the Americans and their goal Mexican General Santa Anna had gathered 30,000 troops, placing nearly all of them at Scott's entrance to the Valley on the east. Seeing this, Scott veered south and marched his army 27 miles over mountain spurs to the southern highway into Mexico City. Although only a hastily-erected line of defense, Mexican fortifications were still in the way. But Lee and the other engineers found a small road going through the Pedregal, an area of volcanic waste, and through this was dispatched two divisions and Magruder's artillery, including Jackson. In the days following, the Mexicans and Americans fought vigorously as the Scott's army pushed toward the Mexican capital. At the Battle of Churubusco (a small stream en route to the City), Magruder was well satisfied with Jackson's brief exploit of heading a charge of three guns. Praising his activity, Magruder said to Scott, "I cannot too highly commend him to the Major-General's favourable consideration."

After heavy fighting, on August 20 Scott's army at last arrived just short of the gates of the city. Scott then proposed an armistice. On September 5 negotiations failed and hostilities resumed. On September 12 the Battle of Chapultepec began, so named for a landmark hill overlooking the southwest route to the city. In one of the most brutal encounters of the war, with nearly every horse killed and huge casualties, Jackson struggled to keep his men from abandoning their position. Almost singlehandedly he and Magruder fired at the Mexican troops until the tide turned.

Then US troops (including the young Ulysses S. Grant) chased Santa Anna all the way back to the City, with Jackson reassembling his guns abreast of the fighting line as they went. On September 14, when Santa Anna abandoned the capital, the war ended for Jackson, and he remained in Mexico City. Santa Anna subsequently attempted – and

General Winfield Scott entering Mexico City. Negotiations to end the war dragged on for another half year, and a treaty of peace was finally signed in mid-1848.

By the end of the fighting in Mexico, when this portrait was made, Lieutenant Thomas J. Jackson had been breveted major, only 18 months after graduation from West Point.

failed – to take Puebla by siege (it was raised October 12). Negotiations dragged through February 1848, and a treaty ending the Mexican War was finally signed June 12, 1848.

Jackson had risen within 18 months of graduation from West Point to the rank of breveted Major. His comrades in arms read like a roster of Who's Who in the War Between the States. Magruder, Joseph Hooker, Irvin McDowell and A. P. Hill were all part of his own regiment. George McClellan, P. G. T. Beauregard, and Gustavus Smith served with Lee. Others included James Shields, John Pope, D. H. Hill, James Longstreet, George Pickett, Fitz-John Porter, Jesse Reno and Richard Ewell.

On June 12 Jackson returned to the United States. From Fort Hamilton, Long Island, he was assigned to Fort Meade, Florida, under Brevet Major William Henry French, his superior by seniority only. "It is doubtful I shall relinquish the military profession, as I am very partial to it," he wrote to Laura, turning down an offer of some money. "All the aid which will be required will be in obtaining fame."

But Florida turned out to be a difficult place to find glory. Jackson soon became embroiled in a petty power struggle with French, and the conflict eventually began to raise questions in army circles about how well Jackson could take orders. To avoid further difficulty, Jackson resigned his commission to accept a professorship at Virginia Military Institute.

As a Professor of Natural Philosophy and artillery tactics

Jackson was by all accounts an uninspired and uninspiring teacher. Indeed, he was called "Tom Fool" by several of the cadets and graduates, and some even demanded his dismissal. In one area only was "Old Jack," as he began to be called, outstanding. At drill, as Thomas M. Semmes, a future colleague and former student, wrote, "The whole man was transported by [imagined] scenes of the actual battlefield."

Lexington welcomed Jackson. He joined the First Presbyterian church, frequented John Lyle's club-like bookstore and, through friends, met two sisters, Eleanor and Margaret Junkin. Jackson courted and, on August 4, 1853, married the younger, Ellie, but 14 months later Ellie died in

childbirth. The downcast Jackson then took a leave of absence from VMI and toured the British Isles and the West Indies. When he returned he slowly began to circulate again in Lexington society. Finally, in July, 1857, he married Mary Anna Morrison – he called her Anna – the daughter of the local Presbyterian minister, and they set up housekeeping in Lexington, bought land for their garden and purchased four domestic slaves. Life now seemed to have settled into a quiet domestic pattern for Jackson, and his youthful dreams of military glory appeared to be fading rapidly away. But history's hold on Thomas Jackson was not to be so easily loosened.

This portrait of the Jackson family at home is probably a work of imagination, in that Jackson's daughter was only six months old when he saw her for the last time.

Above right: *A VMI cadet in battle dress. When Virginia seceded, Jackson led a corps of cadets to Richmond for training.*

Stars and Bars Over Bull Run

John Brown's raid on Harper's Ferry in 1859 signaled the beginning of difficult times for the Union. It prompted Northern abolitionists to hail Brown as a martyr-hero, but for Southerners (including Jackson) it heightened the fear of slave insurrection and further Federal encroachment on states' rights. The increasingly divided nation watched the upcoming elections in 1860 with growing aprehension. Eloquent Stephen Douglas, Democratic Senator from Illinois, was not tough enough for pro-slavery voters, and Southern radicals split from the Democratic Party, organizing their own convention and nominating John Breckinridge. On November 6, 1860, anti-slavery Republican Party candidate Abraham Lincoln defeated Douglas, Breckinridge and John Bell (of the Constitutional Union Party) for the presidency.

Parading under their new flag in April 1861, the men of Company K of the 4th Georgia Volunteers were typical of the untried army of the Confederate States.

In the alarmed South secessionist sentiment now truly began to fulminate.

Jackson, like most southerners, had voted for Breckinridge. Regarding slavery, Jackson, said his wife Anna, "found the institution a responsible and troublesome one, and I have heard him say that he would prefer to see the negroes free, but he . . . accepted slavery, as it existed in the South, not as a thing desirable in itself, but as allowed by Providence for ends which it was not his business to determine."

With Lincoln waiting in the wings and Buchanan a lame-duck president, the South held its breath. On December 27, US Major Robert Anderson took over Fort Sumter, situated 3.3 miles offshore from Charleston, South Carolina. The South debated hotly about their next course of action.

On December 29, 1860, Jackson wrote to Laura: "I am strong for the Union at present, and if things become no worse I hope to continue so." But he shared the Southern view that a state's internal affairs were not the Union's business, nor should it "endeavor to subjugate us, and thus excite our slaves to servile insurrection in which our families

Above: *The target of Union guns throughout the Civil War, the Confederate flag flew over Fort Sumter until February 17, 1865.*

Right: *The special edition of the Charleston* Mercury *announcing South Carolina's secession on December 20, 1860.*

caught up in the widespread enthusiasm for secession that followed the retaking of Sumter, immediately volunteered his services to the new Confederate state of Virginia. On April 21 Richmond accepted his offer.

Awarded the rank of colonel, Jackson brought a corps of VMI cadets, several cannon and some ammunition into Richmond and began training new Virginia recruits. After a few days he was transferred to Harper's Ferry to command a heterogeneous crew officially known as "The Army of the Shenandoah." These recruits consisted of 4500 southern citizens – plantation owners, city men in newly tailored uniforms, hardscrabble farmers and even backwoodsmen in homespun and coonskin hats. Their arms included everything from Bowie knives to shotguns. Nevertheless, Jackson was back in his element. He immediately started reorganizing the troops and imposing discipline, and he saw to it that any excess "luxury" items were sent right back home. As one company member complained, "He considered a gum cloth, a blanket, a tooth brush and forty rounds of cartridges as the full equipment of a gentleman soldier."

These measures made him no more popular than he had

CHARLESTON
MERCURY
EXTRA:

Passed unanimously at 1.15 o'clock, P. M. December 20th, 1860.

AN ORDINANCE

To dissolve the Union between the State of South Carolina and other States united with her under the compact entitled "The Constitution of the United States of America."

We, the People of the State of South Carolina, in Convention assembled, do declare and ordain, and it is hereby declared and ordained,

That the Ordinance adopted by us in Convention, on the twenty-third day of May, in the year of our Lord one thousand seven hundred and eighty-eight, whereby the Constitution of the United States of America was ratified, and also, all Acts and parts of Acts of the General Assembly of this State, ratifying amendments of the said Constitution, are hereby repealed; and that the union now subsisting between South Carolina and other States, under the name of "The United States of America," is hereby dissolved.

THE
UNION
IS
DISSOLVED!

will be murdered without quarter or mercy." That was grounds for war, according to Jackson.

On April 14, 1861, Confederate General Pierre Gustave Toutant Beauregard, Jackson's old Mexican War colleague, attacked and reclaimed Fort Sumter for the South. On hearing the news several VMI cadets took over the flagstaff in the center of Lexington, substituting Virginia's flag for the Stars and Stripes and placing it under armed guard. VMI's Commandant reined in his cadets before they confronted local challengers; and Jackson met his young charges as they returned with a terse and, for this unpopular and bumbling teacher, effective speech. Reprimanding them gently, he concluded, "Time may come when your state will need your services; and if that time does come, then draw your swords and throw away the scabbards."

When Beauregard first opened fire on Fort Sumter some Americans still hoped for peace. In office only since March, Lincoln quickly requested recruits from Virginia to help "suppress insurrection." Governor Letcher refused, believing the Federal Government had no right to interfere in the internal affairs of the seceded states, much less garrison Federal troops at Fort Sumter. The Stars and Bars went up in Richmond on April 17, and soon after in the capitals of Arkansas, Tennessee and North Carolina. Thomas Jackson, been at VMI, but from these recruits Jackson ultimately shaped an elite force whose members would soon credit Jackson for their success in battle. His First Brigade, which would before long be called the "Stonewall Brigade," consisted of 2611 men: like Confederate troops in general, farmers and laborers were the most numerous in terms of professions represented. (The least represented in the brigade were constables, ministers and postmasters.) Of the majority, many were illiterate and many were non-English foreign-born (mostly German and Irish or Scotch-Irish). A remarkable characteristic was how many in the brigade were interrelated – whole groups of cousins, sons and other close relatives had signed on together. To no one's surprise, outside of a handful of personal slaves, black people were hardly in evidence.

No one, North or South, seemed to think the war would take long: among the Federal troops there were many three-month recruits naively hoping for quick victory, and the atmosphere in Southern capitals was more like that of holiday than of war. "All we ask is to be left alone," said Confederate President Jefferson Davis. The Confederate strate-

gists had no plans to invade the North, but expected to use the Confederacy's fewer men, shorter supply lines and easier means of communication to create an impregnable defense.

In May, 1861, the Confederate congress voted to move their capital from Montgomery, Alabama, to Richmond, Virginia. One effect of this was that Manassas, about 75 miles north of Richmond, immediately became essential to the defense of the city. Manassas was a transportation center where, at Manassas Junction in the center of the region, two railroads joined: the Orange and Alexandria ran North-South, connecting Washington and Richmond, and the Manassas Gap Railroad extended west through the Blue Ridge mountains to the Shenandoah valley. Close by, an important road, the Warrenton Turnpike, went through Centreville to Alexandria and Washington.

Midway between the gentle hills and green-treed farmlands of Centreville and Manassas was an easy-going stream, Bull Run Creek. It was to this creek, in July, that the South moved its defensive troops, under the overall command of Brigadier General P. G. T. Beauregard. He had

Left: *Variety of uniforms worn by officers and men of the Confederate Army.*

Below: *The 25 generals of the Confederate Army with Robert E. Lee. Jackson, who was commissioned brigadier general on June 17, 1861, stands in the front row at Lee's left.*

Right: *At the First Battle of Bull Run General Jackson took up a position with his brigade on the strategic Henry House Hill. It was here, standing fast in the battle, that he acquired the nickname "Stonewall."*

Below: *Generals McClellan and McDowell, with the US Fifth Cavalry, cross Bull Run at Blackburn's Ford, one of seven fords that crossed the stream.*

never commanded a large body of troops in the field, nor had his opposing general, Brigadier General Irvin McDowell, another Mexican War veteran. Nevertheless, with his 22,000 recruits Beauregard prepared to fight, and, to be safe, he had asked Brigadier General Joseph E. Johnston, to provide reinforcements as needed via the Manassas Gap Railroad. Under Johnston's command was Jackson and his brigade, now battle-ready.

On July 16 Beauregard received word from Mrs. Rose O'Neal Greenhow, a Confederate spy living in Washington, that McDowell was coming. When he arrived, McDowell met what appeared to be a nearly inpenetrable line of Con-

federate defenses along Bull Run, and he began to wonder if a decisive battle was possible. Meanwhile, civilians and dignitaries from Washington were jamming the roads carrying picnic baskets and opera glasses with all the lightheartedness of a crowd at a country fair. Though that may seem incongruous now, a Federal soldier commented, "We thought it wasn't a bad idea to have the great men from Washington come out to see us thrash the Rebs."

The route that Jackson traveled to Manassas had been eventful. At the end of June, when they were ordered to march southward by Johnston, Jackson's men had been fidgety for a real battle, and as a roving reporter for *Harper's*

Weekly noted, they were "under very strict discipline but seemed discontented and not in very good condition." Ahead of them, on July 2, Jackson's associate, Confederate cavalry Colonel J. E. B. (Jeb) Stuart sighted Federal Troops heading south, and the Rebels skirmished almost bloodlessly against Union roops under General Robert Patterson until the Federals withdrew. On July 3 Jackson was promoted to Brigadier General, and then he and his troops settled in Winchester, a key Shenandoah town south of Harper's Ferry to wait for the next move.

At noon on July 18 Jackson sent each of his regimental commanders orders to evacuate Winchester: this was in response to Beauregard's call for Johnston's reinforcements at Manassas. "With the Confederate banners waving, the bands playing, and the bayonets gleaming in the sun. . . . Many of the companies were made up of mere boys, but their earnest and joyous faces were fully as reassuring as the martial music was inspiriting," wrote one witness to their departure, Mrs. Cornelia MacDonald.

Jackson's units arrived by rail, clinging to cars that pulled into Manassas late in the afternoon of July 20. The next day, at 4:30 in the morning of July 21, cannons began to grumble. Jackson put his troops at right angles to Bull Run at Henry House Hill overlooking the Federals pressing towards Matthews Hill. He immediately sent word to General Bernard Bee, commanding in the sector, that he was on the field. Amid thunderous noise, bursting shells and men crying out loud, "Oh Lord, have mercy!" the soldiers settled in to man their defenses. But by about two in the afternoon General Bee was shouting to Jackson, "General! They are beating us back!"

"Then, sir, we will give them the bayonet," replied Jackson, ordering the First Brigade to hold their position below the crest of the hill. Bee, rallying his retreating men, stood up in his stirrups and shouted to them, "Look! There is Jackson standing like a stone wall! Rally behind the Virginians!" At that moment Jackson acquired his nickname, but shortly thereafter Bee lost his life. Then Jackson's men tumbled over the crest of the hill and fired into the face of an unprepared line of Union soldiers, letting loose the famous "Rebel Yell" over the ear-splitting noise of battle. The attack was conducted exactly according to Jackson's plan. "Order the men to stand up," Jackson had said. "Reserve your fire until they come within fifty yards, then fire and give them the bayonet; and, when you charge, yell like furies!"

As the fighting came down to hand-to-hand combat, fresh Confederate troops under General E. Kirby arrived, and it was this that ultimately produced an overwhelming Southern victory. But it was the Stonewall Brigade, as well as it's leader, that had established the most enduring reputation at Bull Run.

Unfortunately for the South, Beauregard did not now employ the follow-up tactic that Jackson, ever since his Mexico days, had considered so essential. Jackson was not permitted to attack the retreating enemy or, as he would have liked, invade Washington. Historians have since suggested that this was one of the outstanding tactical blunders of the war.

Dismayed at the carnage and at the defeat at Bull Run, one Union observer wrote: "We have undertaken to make war without in the least knowing how." It would have been a good time for the Confederacy to push that advantage. But, as this first grim encounter showed, the war was not going to be either short or easy for either side.

Left: *A quarter of a century after the First Battle of Bull Run, an artist created this view of the Union retreat. Jackson was not permitted to pursue the fleeing troops.*

Overleaf: *The ruins of Henry House atop the hill where Stonewall Jackson's troops distinguished themselves. Jackson won praise all over the Confederacy for his performance at Bull Run, and on October 7, 1861 he was commissioned major general.*

The Shenandoah

The war, formless at first, gradually began to take on strategic shape. Jefferson Davis, Jackson's Commander-in-Chief, stubbornly held to his defensive strategy, while the Union, somewhat sobered by the Bull Run defeat, renewed its offense with more matériel and vastly superior numbers. One aspect of Union strategy sought to divide Virginia right down the Shenandoah Valley, the Confederate breadbasket, and press towards Richmond. (This conformed to the popular rallying cry, "On to Richmond!") Another, longer-range and more feared, part of Union strategy was "Scott's Anaconda Plan," a serpentine squeeze of the Confederates by the Union Navy on the Atlantic side and Union regulars on the Mississippi side.

A matter of particular concern to the South was the unstable situation in western Virginia. In late August of 1861 the western counties of Virginia had broken away and formed the independent state of West Virginia, and it appeared that the new state would join the Union. The countryside was crawling with Federal soldiers, and even Jackson himself could not ignore the strong Union sentiment openly voiced there. But Stonewall hoped that his birthplace, the land where his mother lay buried, might still be won for the Con-

Jefferson Davis preferred an army command and hoped to lead the Army of the Confederacy. He reluctantly accepted his selection as provisional president of the Confederate States and took office on February 18, 1861.

General George B. McClellan, who succeeded McDowell after Bull Run, was assigned the task of building a Union army that could conquer Virginia. A fine trainer of men, he seemed to Lincoln to be timid and overcautious.

federacy. Indeed, the South wanted to win not only militarily in border states like West Virginia, they hoped to win as well by encouraging Confederate sympathies in these areas.

Although Jackson understood the importance of the western Virginia theater, in the autumn of 1861 his thoughts were still firmly fixed on the east and the possibility of an offensive against Washington. He could confidently say when, after Bull Run, Lincoln replaced McDowell with Jackson's old West Point classmate George McClellan: "McClellan, with his army of recruits, will not attempt to come out against us this autumn. If we remain inactive they will have greatly the advantage over us next spring." He continued to press his case into late October, 1861, when he asked his new CO, G. W. Smith, to intervene with the South's War Office in favor of invading the North. No. Smith replied, the Office had already rejected the idea.

On November 4, 1861, Jackson was sent instead to command the army of the Shenandoah Valley District, a position at this time remote from any possibility of invading the North. Sadly he obeyed, though he hated to leave his brigade: "You are the First Brigade in the affections of your general, and I hope by your future deeds and bearing you will be handed down to posterity as the First Brigade in this our second War of Independence. Farewell!"

On November 5 Jackson set up headquarters at Winchester, a town at the northern end of the Shenandoah Valley, thus spoiling the plans of the Union's General William Rosecrans, who had hoped to occupy the town himself, so as to guard the Baltimore and Ohio Railway. Now the Confederate front went from Fredericksburg, on the Rappahannock River south of Washington, D.C., to Jackson's Winchester post on the Opequon.

Upon arrival Jackson saw that Valley defenses were under-staffed; he immediately telegraphed Richmond for reinforcements, including – by special request – his old brigade. Destined to be with him till his death, Stonewall's First Brigade arrived by rail in Strasburg on November 10 and, with other troops, marched to Kernstown, to Winchester and then to Camp Stephenson (nicknamed "New Centerville") four and a half miles outside of town.

The weather immediately turned foul: freezing rain, sleet, ice and muck made Jackson's men not only miserable but sick. Many contracted influenza and measles; others got the

"Virginia quickstep," as they dubbed the debilitating bouts of diarrohea. Morale began to suffer, as did discipline. Fortunately, at this time Jackson's Brigade got a new brigade commander, the famed Indian fighter Brigadier General Richard B. Garnett, who established a benevolent rapport with his new charges quickly and raised troop spirits at a difficult time.

Believing that "an active winter's campaign is less liable to produce disease than a sedentary life by campfires in winter quarters," Stonewall planned to take the town of Romney, a strategic point for maintaining communications between Federals in the eastern and western regions of Virginia. He waited only for a break in the frigid weather that had settled over them.

The weather turned at the year's end. Following Jackson's habit of early morning, often highly secretive marches, the troops set out on New Year's Day, 1862, at 5:00 AM. Almost immediately the weather turned foul once more. Already hungry and exhausted, the men occupied the town of Bath en route, failed to cross the river near Hancock and then turned south towards Romney and the worst night

of their campaign. At one in the afternoon on January 14, Stonewall's army reached an abandoned Romney. "When we marched into town," wrote one member of that campaign, "every soldier's clothing was a solid cake of ice, and icicles two inches long hanging from the hair and whiskers of every man." Many fell en route. Worse still, Old Jack seemed oblivious to the misery in the ranks – misery so acute that reports of it even reached Federal ears. "We have reliable information that he sent back over 1200 frozen and sick men during the four days he lay [at Romney]. People . . . say that his sick and disabled fill every house from Bath to Winchester and that many amputations have taken place from frost-bite," wrote Union General Seth Williams of Stonewall's suffering troops.

Quartering his own brigade in Winchester, Jackson left a subordinate, General William W. Loring, to cover the Romney area. The latter promptly petitioned the Confederate Secretary of War, Judah Benjamin, for a transfer from Romney. Jackson, who was already distressed that Lee, assigned to West Virginia almost immediately after Bull Run, had lost Jackson's home territory at the Battle of Cheat

Left: *The Confederate First Virginia Cavalry at a halt, sketched in the field by Civil War artist Alfred R. Waud. Confederate cavalry proved most effective when employed to conduct raids, harass enemy supply lines, create diversions and gather information.*

Far left: *Jackson's infantry, vastly outnumbered by Union troops in the Shenandoah, tormented the Federals with rapid marches, gaining the nickname "foot cavalry."*

Below: *A Confederate picket posted to guard against a surprise attack.*

Mountain early in September, recalled Loring, as ordered by Richmond, and then tendered his resignation on January 31, 1862. "With such interference in my command, I cannot expect to be of much service in the field," he began. Confederate brass begged him to stay. Stonewall wrote Davis that he would remain only if it was considered dangerous for the South if he were to leave: in effect, he was telling his civilian government to leave him alone. It did, and Jackson withdrew his resignation.

As the 1862 campaign began, the Confederates felt well positioned, with Jackson in full command of the approach to the Shenandoah Valley, "Uncle Joe" Johnston's forces centered around Manassas and Theophilus Holmes' troops stationed to the east near Fredericksburg. Then, early in March, Union troops began to move against the Confederates – McClellan against Johnston and Holmes and General Nathaniel Banks advancing southwest on Harper's Ferry to push Jackson out of the Shenandoah. Thirty-eight thousand Federals now threatened Winchester, including 2000 cavalry and 80 pieces of artillery.

On March 11 Jackson held a council of war with his officers. They had already decided to evacuate Winchester, but rather than just leave it to Banks and his Federal troops, Jackson now planned to circle to Newtown and return to attack Banks by night. In the event, however, the plan failed because Jackson's officers moved too slowly to use the cover of darkness. "That is the last council of war I will ever hold!" fumed Jackson, and he kept his word. Now the Federals under Banks seemed securely in position to bottle up the Confederates in the Shenandoah.

The savage winter had so reduced his troop strength that by March Jackson had but three brigades, or about 4600 men, left. Yet despite his pleas, President Davis refused to spare him any of Johnston's or Hill's units. To make matters worse, events elsewhere were conspiring to make the Shenandoah theater more strategically important than ever before.

Union General George McClellan thought that he had at last found a war-winning strategy. In his new spring offensive, rather than trying to capture the Confederate capital by sending his army due south along the well-defended direct route from Washington to Richmond, he would in-

Left: *Union General Nathaniel Banks commanded 20,000 men in the Winchester area against Jackson's approximately 4200. Banks was routed.*

Right: *Confederate General Joseph E. Johnston, his army held down by McClellan, could spare no troops to reinforce Jackson's small force in the Shenandoah.*

stead transport his forces by sea to Fortress Monroe, on the Virginia coast *southeast* of Richmond, and then move on the city via the lightly-defended area known as the Peninsula that lay between the York and James rivers. Banks would remain in the Valley to deal with Jackson, and in case of trouble he could be backed up by a 30,000-man corps under Irvin McDowell that would be held in the vicinity of Washington. Once the threat in the Valley had been removed, McDowell, and possibly Banks as well, would join McClellan in the Peninsula. In other words, both the speed and the amount of reinforcement that McClellan could expect would depend on Jackson's ability to remain in the Valley and mount a potential threat to Washington or Maryland.

At the outset the Federals did not take Jackson's force very seriously. Indeed, Banks had left only his subordinate, General James Shields, to cover the vital Potomac crossing at Harper's Ferry, the B & O Railway and the Chesapeake Canal. Jackson at once grasped the situation and decided to go over to the offensive.

On March 22 Jackson's cavalry, under Turner Ashby, skirmished with Shields' pickets just south of Winchester. The following battle at Kernstown, on March 23, was brutal, in part because Ashby's intelligence underestimated Federal opposition: not an exiting fragment, but an entire Federal division lay in wait for the Rebels. Jackson's units lost some 700 out of only 4200 engaged, and the morale of his men sank. But the Confederate strategy worked: The Federals now assigned three of Banks' divisions to the Shenandoah – troops that McClellan would have been glad to have with him on the Peninsula.

In the weeks following Kernstown, Banks' larger force made Jackson move up (southward) the Valley. When Jackson learned that Federal General John Frémont was going to bring his units across the Alleghenies to reinforce Banks' force, on April 30 he set off with his own brigades, and after marching 92 miles in four days, his units challenged a completely confused Frémont at McDowell, on the edge of the Allegheny Mountains. In the ensuing battle the Confederates lost some 498 men to the Union's 246 casualties, but Jackson had once again derailed the Federal timetable.

By this time Jackson knew very well that his survival depended on his willingness to remain on the move. How else could his army – now reinforced but still only 16,000 men – hold off three Federal armies? If they could ever pin Jackson down to one place and one pitched battle, his force could be annihilated. So on May 15 Jackson set off with his troops northward. In the last 16 hours they covered 26 miles before surfacing on May 23 at Front Royal.

As one admiring account put it, Jackson "popped out of his hole" at Front Royal, and in three hours the Confederates had all but massacred the Federals. Jackson's force had suffered only 50 casualties to the Federals' 904, and the Confederates now controlled every road west and north from Front Royal. Banks, in dismay, scurried for Winchester, hoping to escape from the Valley.

Using helpful information from a Confederate spy, Belle Boyd, Jackson routed the Federals at Winchester on May 25. In a single day the *New York Herald* was confidently announcing "Fall of Richmond" (what the Union fully anticipated) in the morning, and that same evening it was reporting that the entire Confederate army was marching towards Washington. The Union was shaken. Over McClellan's objections, Lincoln now ordered McDowell into the Valley.

On May 28 Jackson advanced to Harper's Ferry. As the result of the ensuing battle he could have taken Harper's Ferry and its stores of munitions, but – inexplicably and perhaps foolishly – he did not. Rather, he returned to Winchester. There he heard that the 12th Georgia had abandoned Front Royal. On the night of May 30 all the Army of the Valley was ordered back to strasburg, not 12 miles from Front Royal. Winchester had to be abandoned.

Jackson had waged a brilliantly effective form of guerrilla warfare. Vastly outnumbered and outarmed, he had tormented Union troops with rapid marches (his troops gained the nickname "foot cavalry") and stealthy tactics. His moves also reflected the "offensive-defensive" strategy expounded by Lee, who in June took command of the Army of Northern Virginia. The enemy couldn't put a large force at every assailable point; the South hadn't a large force; so Lee moved his troops like chesspieces. Yet, "Some partial encroachments of the enemy we must expect," said Lee. The sacrifice of Winchester was one of those expected events.

But the real importance of Jackson's Valley Campaign lay in the reinforcements it denied McClellan in the Peninsula. Just how much of the ultimate failure of the Peninsular strategy can be attributed to this has been debated by historians ever since, but that Jackson contributed mightily to McClellan's downfall is beyond doubt.

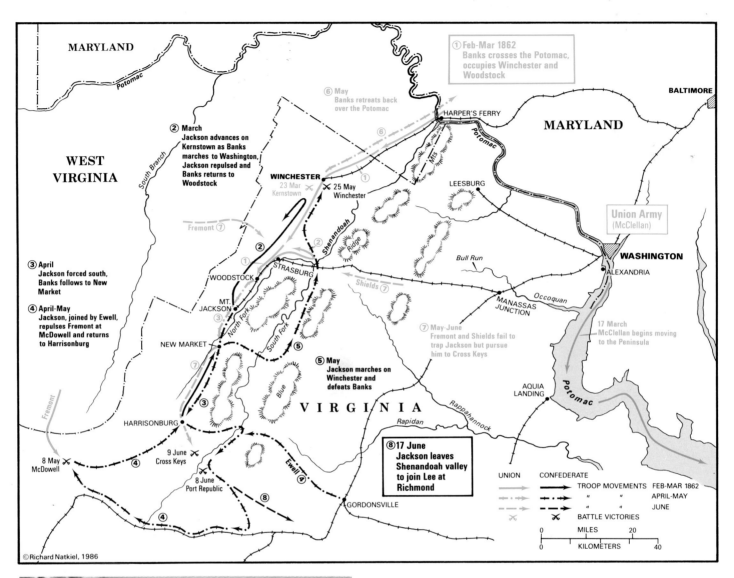

MARYLAND

Potomac

BALTIMORE

① Feb–Mar 1862
Banks crosses the Potomac,
occupies Winchester and
Woodstock

⑥ May
Banks retreats back
over the Potomac

HARPER'S FERRY

MARYLAND

WEST
VIRGINIA

South Branch

② March
Jackson advances on
Kernstown as Banks
marches to Washington,
Jackson repulsed and
Banks returns to
Woodstock

WINCHESTER
23 Mar ✗ Kernstown
✗ 25 May Winchester

LEESBURG

Union Army
(McClellan)

Fremont ⑦

②

Shenandoah
Ridge

Bull Run

WASHINGTON
ALEXANDRIA

③ April
Jackson forced south,
Banks follows to New
Market

④ April–May
Jackson, joined by Ewell,
repulses Fremont at
McDowell and returns
to Harrisonburg

WOODSTOCK

STRASBURG

MT.
JACKSON

North Fork

①

③

Shields ⑦

MANASSAS
JUNCTION

Occoquan

⑦ May–June
Fremont and Shields fail to
trap Jackson but pursue
him to Cross Keys

17 March
McClellan begins moving
to the Peninsula

NEW MARKET

South Fork

⑤

⑤ May
Jackson marches on
Winchester and
defeats Banks

Blue

VIRGINIA

Rappahannock

AQUIA
LANDING

Potomac

Fremont

HARRISONBURG

③

Rapidan

⑦

Ewell

8 May ✗
McDowell

9 June ✗
Cross Keys

④

8 June
Port Republic

④

⑧ 17 June
Jackson leaves
Shenandoah valley
to join Lee at
Richmond

UNION   CONFEDERATE

⟶ TROOP MOVEMENTS FEB–MAR 1862

"   "   APRIL–MAY

"   "   JUNE

✗   ✗ BATTLE VICTORIES

0   MILES   20

0   KILOMETERS   40

⑧

GORDONSVILLE

©Richard Natkiel, 1986

Above: *An annotated map
of Jackson's Valley
campaign, which frustrated
the Union advance on
Richmond and denied
McClellan reinforcements
in the Peninsula. The map
traces troop movements
from Banks' occupation of
Winchester (1) to his defeat
(5) and retreat (6), and
Jackson's withdrawal (7-8)
from the Shenandoah
Valley.*

Left: *Confederate spy Belle
Boyd, working from Front
Royal, Virginia, provided
Jackson with intelligence
on Union operations in the
Shenandoah Valley. She
was imprisoned twice, in
1862 and 1863, but was
released for lack of
evidence.*

Right: *Union General Irvin
McDowell, the first leader
of the Army of the
Potomac, lost his command
after the defeat at First Bull
Run. Following Banks'
defeat by Jackson, and
over McClellan's
objections, President
Lincoln ordered General
McDowell to push Jackson
from the Valley.*

"On to Richmond"

After Jackson's wily tactics in the Shenandoah Valley made a laughing stock of Union General Banks, a common jingle appeared in newspapers all over the South:

> Whilst Butler plays his silly pranks,
> And closes up New Orleans banks,
> Our Stonewall Jackson, with more cunning,
> Keeps Yankee Banks forever running.

But that was when Jackson had free reign in the Valley. Now Lee wanted to stop using Jackson to divert the Federals in the Shenandoah and use him in a major assault against McClellan before the latter got to Richmond. According to the plan, Lee would place 25,000 Rebel troops between McClellan's forces – en route up the York River – and Rich-

mond; and he would put 47,000 near Mechanicsville on the Union right flank.

As Lee moved his troops into positions Jackson was retreating from Winchester with the intention of engaging two Union forces, those of Frémont and Shields, and keeping them separate and weakened. Literally burning all bridges behind him as he went south, Jackson reached Port Republic on June 6. General Richard Ewell, one of his officers, hung back strategically, four miles northwest at Cross Keys.

Port Republic, a small village, was big in strategic value to the Confederates. It was situated right in the angle where the North and South Forks of the Shenandoah converged, and two important roads met there. Controlling Port Republic meant controlling the Valley; and it was here, once more,

Below: *General Jackson in an engraving of 1861. The hero of the Valley Campaign now headed toward Richmond to join Lee at Mechanicsville.*

Right: *Mechanicsville, Va., where the second of the Seven Days' Battles took place. Jackson arrived too late to take part in the action.*

that Jackson's tenacity spurred the troops on to victory.

On June 8, no sooner than a courier had informed Jackson that Federals were pouring into Port Republic, a cannon roared in the stillness. Determined to hold the bridge to the village, Jackson charged through a fusilade of bullets to urge his men to fire on bluecoats whom the Rebels had decided were their own men in stolen Union uniforms. A hostile volley from the misidentified men proved that Jackson's instincts were correct, and the battle was on.

After a vigorous fight at Cross Keys, Ewell had successfully routed Frémont's forces by nightfall of June 8. As he moved towards Jackson, he found on the 9th that Jackson's men were caught in a wheat field under heavy artillery fire. The Confederates' artillery commander and his "Parrott" battery could not return it. Though Ewell arrived soon, the Brigade retreated into the woods as fellow graycoats began to fall. Dismayed, Jackson galloped into the melee shouting, "The Stonewall Brigade never retreats! Follow me!" Three brutal charges later the Federals gave in to a deadly cross-

fire – on their flank from the Stonewall Brigade and on the front from a Louisiana Contingent. The Federals then removed themselves from the battle.

As a result of the battles at Cross Keys and Port Republic, the Federal strategy had to be revamped. No longer would the Union try to take the Shenandoah Valley and no longer would it try to wipe out Jackson on his own ground. The Confederates had suffered heavy casualties during the Valley Campaign, but Old Jack had defeated three Union armies 60,000 strong with only a few more than 16,000 men.

As early as June 6 Jackson had written to Lee that he could be out of the Valley and near Mechanicsville in two days. After Port Republic his forces went into camp on the 12th, and shortly thereafter Lee ordered Jackson to come out of the Valley and join in the defense of Richmond.

On June 17 long gray lines left the Valley through Brown's Gap as Jackson, now gathering about him 18,500 troops, headed for Richmond and the Federals' rear guard. Scheduled to meet Lee's troops on June 25 just north of Mechan-

icsville (itself just outside Richmond), Jackson, despite his hard driving, was uncharacteristically late at the first of what would become known as the Seven Days' Battles.

The Battle of Oak Grove on June 25, which some accounts barely rate as a battle, resulted in the Federals taking the Confederate position there. Then, on the 26th, the Battle of Mechanicsville ensued. Confederate General A. P. Hill held out as best as he could, for Jackson did not arrive until three that afternoon, too late to take part in the action. "Ah, General, I am very glad to see you. I had hoped to be with you before," snapped Lee.

"Yes, sir, no excuse, sir," replied Jackson. What he did not add was that he had had no usable maps of the Chickhominy River country around the southern capital.

On June 27 A. P. Hill and James Longstreet moved on Gaines' Mill, where the Union's General Fitz-John Porter had retreated. Again Jackson was delayed by taking a roundabout route to the battlefield that got him there well after 4:00 PM. Nevertheless, his arrival was a great psychological boost for the troops already engaged. "Jackson's men! The Valley men are here!" was the shout up and down the gray

Left: *Confederate Major General Richard Stoddart Ewell commanded a division of troops under General Stonewall Jackson throughout the Seven Days' Battles.*

Below: *The Parrott rifle was one of the first rifled field guns used by the US army. Such artillery figured heavily in the attempted Union assault on Richmond.*

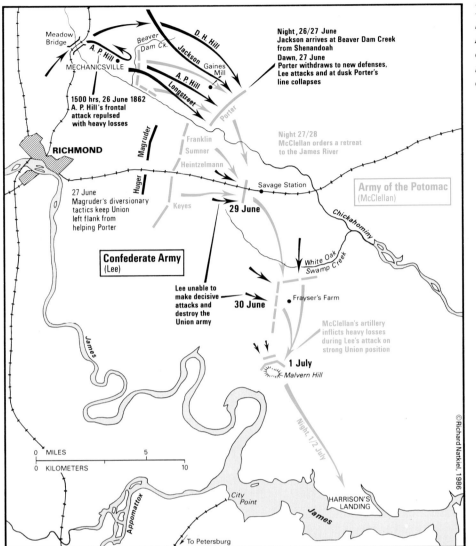

Left: *Map of troop movements in the Seven Days' Battles, the successful defense of the approaches to the Confederate capital of Richmond.*

Labels within map:

Meadow Bridge
A. P. Hill
MECHANICSVILLE
Beaver Dam Ck.
D. H. Hill
Jackson
A. P. Hill
Gaines Mill
Longstreet
Porter

Night, 26/27 June
Jackson arrives at Beaver Dam Creek from Shenandoah
Dawn, 27 June
Porter withdraws to new defenses,
Lee attacks and at dusk Porter's line collapses

1500 hrs, 26 June 1862
A. P. Hill's frontal attack repulsed with heavy losses

RICHMOND

Magruder
Franklin
Sumner
Heintzelmann
Huger
Keyes

Night 27/28
McClellan orders a retreat to the James River

Savage Station

Army of the Potomac
(McClellan)

27 June
Magruder's diversionary tactics keep Union left flank from helping Porter

29 June

Chickahominy

Confederate Army
(Lee)

Lee unable to make decisive attacks and destroy the Union army

30 June

White Oak Swamp Creek

Frayser's Farm

McClellan's artillery inflicts heavy losses during Lee's attack on strong Union position

1 July
Malvern Hill

Night 1/2 July

James

0 MILES 5
0 KILOMETERS 10

© Richard Natkiel, 1986

Appomattox

City Point

HARRISON'S LANDING

James

To Petersburg

lines as they plunged into the conflict. General Charles Winder, now in command of the old Stonewall Brigade, led three regiments into a swampy area just short of a clearing. It was smoky with artillery fire, and they entered the fray with a high-pitched rebel yell. The story goes that the yell made Jackson jerk a half-sucked lemon from his mouth – it was a habit to which he was addicted – and raise hand and lemon high, cheering his men on.

It would later be claimed that in this campaign Jackson was mentally drained by exhaustion, that he had to be steadied on his horse, Little Sorrel, that he could barely lift his fork to his mouth, that his servant undressed him, boots and all, without waking him. But it is also true that Jackson always had a difficult time whenever someone else was giving the orders. To quote D. H. Hill, "Jackson's genius never shone when he was under the command of another. It seemed to him he was shrouded and paralyzed."

With or without Jackson, Lee's tactics seemed to be working well. At the Battle of Gaines' Mill (June 27-28), though McClellan's flank survived the Confederate onslaught, McClellan became disheartened by the lethal nature of the opposition. Jackson's regiment, led by John Hood, had fought doggedly in a field thick with grapeshot, cannister and shell. Slowly the Union troops fell back, and by the morning of he 28th no Union formation was visible

north of the Chickahominy. Thus, in a battle of nerves, the Rebels had gained the upper hand, even though the Federals had made it more difficult for the Confederates by using the very "flying artillery" that Jackson had so admired in the Mexican War.

It was now evident that McClellan was heading for Hamilton's Landing on the James River via White Oak Swamp. Once at the James he would have the protection of Union gunboats anchored in the river. As there was only one bridge across the swamp, however, his progress was bound to be slow. It was hoped that Jackson might be able to intercept him, but the Grapevine Bridge that Old Jack had to cross had been severely damaged and had to be rebuilt. Again, Jackson was delayed, and McClellan got over the White Oak bridge that night at the cost of his field hospital and some supplies.

Jackson's troops then veered off into the woods, taking numerous prisoners, and stopped in mid-afternoon on the south side at White Oak Swamp. But from there, Jackson refused to budge, even though everyone could hear General James Longstreet and Powell Hill's troops battling in the distance at Frayser's Farm. Supposedly, Jackson overheard some of his men wondering why Stonewall had not joined them; the General growled, "If General Lee had wanted me at Frayser's Farm, he would have sent for me!"

The Battle of Malvern Hill, fought on July 1, brought the Seven Days' Battles to an end. There McClellan assembled his full force and appeared to hold off the Confederates with his superior ordnance. William Poague and Joe Carpenter, the two Confederate captains who directed the Brigade's modest artillery, tried for six hours to move Federal batteries from Malvern Hill. Once the Federals had located Carpenter's range, they poured a torrent of shot upon him: in sheer quantity, it was, he said, "the most severe fire I think I ever experienced." One gunner, four hundred yards to the rear, was resting against an oak tree when a ball came tearing through the 30-inch trunk and decapitated him.

On July 1 Lee cancelled his orders for a general attack, thinking the Union was retreating once more. He did, however, send a unit in pursuit of what he thought was a rear guard. But the Confederates were once more repulsed, and once more they incurred numerous casualties. Jackson's Brigade inched forward and, as night fell, a jumble of soldiers, some not even able to tell friend from foe, exchanged fire after dusk. Lee anticipated another encounter; but Jackson, who knew his old classmate well, correctly predicted that McClellan now really would retreat. The Confederates moved out on July 2 to find that the Yankees had slipped away during the night.

During the ensuing chase Jackson, as usual, drove his troops unmercifully, though they gave him their utmost loyalty. As McClellan's men retreated toward Harrison's Landing the Brigade was close behind until withering fire from the Yankee ships in the river stopped them. General Charles Winder, commanding the Stonewall Brigade in the field, sent a message to Jackson that his men were fearful of the shells. Jackson's reply was brief: "Tell General Winder that I am as much afraid of the shells as his men, but to continue to advance." Winder intervened again; clearly, the men were exhausted. At last, and reluctantly, Jackson ordered the men to go into encampment.

For the Confederates the Seven Days was a victory, but not a decisive one. Although Jackson exultantly and accurately telegraphed his wife, Anna, that "Richmond is saved, by God's provenance," the Federal army remained intact. Lee was in fact bitterly disappointed that McClellan should have been allowed to get to the James River unscathed. But at least the Federals did not renew their offensive. McClellan's force remained at Harrison's Landing until August 3, and then Lincoln ordered the Union's Army of the Potomac out of the Peninsula. Now the only Yankees within 100 miles of Richmond were prisoners.

Artillery batteries of the Federal Army of the Potomac pouring canister shot into the Confederate ranks at the Battle of Gaines' Mill (June 27-28, 1862).

Left: *Confederate General James Longstreet, whom Lee called "my old warhorse," reinforced Jackson's troops at Gaines' Mill.*

Above: *McClellan's Sixth Corps retreating from the Chickahominy in the early morning hours of Sunday June 29, from a sketch made in the field at the time. The regiment shown marching is the 16th New York, which, with its men in straw hats, made a conspicuous target and suffered heavy losses.*

Overleaf: *As McClellan's Federal troops fell back from Gaines' Mill, Jackson had to pause in his pursuit to rebuild the badly damaged Grapevine Bridge across the Chickahominy River.*

Jackson vs Pope

In the Seven Days campaign Jackson's behavior had belied his reputation as a brilliant and daring soldier, and certainly he failed to win the confidence of his commander in chief, Robert E. Lee, who now led the Confederate armies. Lee had already had some doubts about Jackson – his tenure at VMI had been troubled at best, and he had shown himself to be a stern Calvinist who would not hesitate to execute his own soldiers for breach of duty. Just after the Seven Days, Jackson had ordered a firing squad to execute three deserters publicly and then had had his division march by the bullet-riddled corpses as "a lesson." Nor did Jackson's initial and almost proletarian contempt for patrician Lee bode well for a good collaboration. Yet Jackson was soon to speak of Lee as "the only man I know whom I would follow blindfold," and in time the combination of Jackson and Lee would become a legend.

On July 17, 1862, while McClellan was still at Harrison's Landing, the Brigade was moved north to Gordonsville in order to meet a new threat: the Federal Army of Virginia, under Major General John Pope, who had marched in from the western front to take his new post. Pope situated himself several miles north of Jackson and near the source of the Rappahannock River, and rumors circulated that he was formidable.

In fact, it seems clear that Lee deliberately sent Stonewall marching back to the Shenandoah (and nearer Washington) primarily to draw McClellan out of the Peninsula. McClellan wrote frantically to Major General H. E. Halleck, the Union's new Secretary of War, about the folly of evacuating the Union forces from Harrison's Landing, but Halleck soon swallowed the bait and did exactly what the Confederates wanted.

Meanwhile, with a paltry 11,000 men, Jackson set out to face the numerous (47,000), though spread out men in Pope's command. Towards the end of July, Lee sent A. P. Hill to Gordonsville in response to a request from Old Jack for reinforcements. All the while the vainglorious Pope was strutting about like an overblown tom. "I have come to

Below: *General Robert E. Lee, who, Jackson said, was "the only man I know whom I would follow blindfold." The two mounted a brilliant campaign against Union General Pope.*

Right: *Union General John Pope sent his Federal Army of Virginia against Lee's much smaller forces but was beaten back repeatedly by Jackson and Longstreet. Pope blamed his junior officers.*

you," he said, addressing his new charges, "from the West, where we have always seen the backs of our enemies [this was a direct slur against McClellan] – from an army whose business it has been to seek the adversary and beat him when found, whose policy has been attack and not defense." His colleagues were not impressed, though most of them swallowed hard and went along with this new commander. Frémont, however, asked to be relieved of his duties and all but retired in protest.

Pope did not restrict his undiplomatic manner to his troops. The Federals under his command forced local civilians in the area to feed them, take oaths of loyalty and repair all damage to roads, bridges and the communications systems. Needless to say, Southerners soon learned to hate him as much as they adored Stonewall.

On the other hand, Pope's spies were far more efficient

than his predecessor's, and he came much closer than McClellan to correctly estimating the size of his foe's army as both the Federals and Confederates made their preparations for the coming battle. Early in August Jeb Stuart staged a series of brilliant raids that rattled Federal scouting parties in the Fredericksburg area to the east, but still Pope bragged about how he would soon be in possession of Gordonsville and its southwestern neighbor, Charlottesville.

Meanwhile, Stonewall's Brigade was growing restive. Their commander, Charles Winder, incurred resentment when he instituted such harsh discipline that even Stonewall, no slouch himself, ordered it undone. In truth, as one Brigade member perceptively wrote, Jackson and Winder "were too much alike to fit exactly."

On August 7 Jackson, with Winder and the Brigade, turned north towards Culpepper. On August 9 they reached

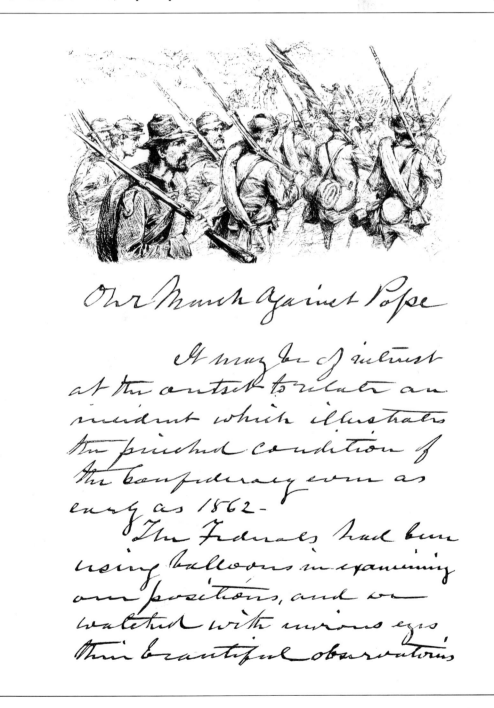

The beginning of a soldier's letter describing a part of the Confederate campaign against Union General Pope.

Slaughter Mountain, a prominence just north of the Rapidan River, separated by about 20 miles from a mountain called the Blue Ridge. One of the most brutal "little" battles of the Civil War, the Battle of Cedar Mountain (as the Blue Ridge was renamed), cost both sides over 3000 casualties. Among the dead was Winder, who, despite his harshness, had shown his men much to respect.

After Winder fell Jackson personally led the men against his old foe, Banks, whom Pope had ordered to move against

Above: *General J. E. B. "Jeb" Stuart, on June 12, took a force of cavalry to scout the Yankees and proceeded to completely circle McClellan's Union army, raiding as he went. This move came to be known as Stuart's First Ride Around McClellan.*

Left: *A Confederate camp in the Virginia woodlands.*

Below: *Union forces at Cedar Mountain, August 9, 1862, the first engagement of the Second Bull Run Campaign. Initially Jackson was driven off by a large force under Banks, but a counterattack by General A. P. Hill pushed the Union army back.*

Stonewall. Banks' attack soon turned into retreat. Waving a standard snatched from its bearer, Jackson rode among his men, urging them on, calling, "My Brigade, where's my Brigade?" as they joined Powell Hill in routing the Federals. The Valley men, one Confederate wrote admiringly, would have followed Stonewall "into the jaws of death itself; nothing could have stopped them and nothing did."

On August 10 Stuart reported that the main body of Pope's army was drawing near. The Confederates withdrew, waited for two days, then withdrew further to Gordonsville

when the Federal force seemed too numerous. As Stuart had observed, the troops that Pope had assembled behind Cedar Mountain numbered nearly 32,000, including cavalry, and another 10,000 were en route.

The Union command still did not know exactly where Jackson had gone after Cedar Mountain. "I don't like Jackson's movements, "McClellan wrote to Halleck, "He will suddenly appear when least expected." Then, on August 22, Jackson's dashing cavalry commander, Jeb Stuart, made a raid on Pope's supply wagons and captured the General's

dispatch book. It contained a treasure trove of military information: positions, projected reinforcements, revisions of strategy and notes to the effect that Pope believed the line along the Rappahannock was still not secure.

The Confederate commanders pored over this material and shaped their plans accordingly. On the 24th Jackson and Lee conferred and, in the words of Brigade member Alexander Hunter, "Lee now determined . . . to send Jackson around in Pope's rear and cut him off from Washington, while he [Lee] would attack in front. Such a step was rash and fraught with many dangers, for Pope, by turning his whole army on Jackson, might overwhelm him before Lee could assist." Hunter added that such a move was considered by Lee only because he had a low opinion of Pope's military skills. "And so," wrote Hunter, "Jackson, with 17,300 rank and file, set off on the morning of the 25th of August from Gordonsville and moved up the western side of the Bull Run Mountains." On the 26th Jackson came

through Thoroughfare Gap with the plains of Manassas before him.

When Jackson's men took the small station of Bristoe, a Federal train to Washington sped by out of the firing range, and thus news of Confederate movement reached the Union capital. Stuart, meanwhile, attacked the Federal supply depot at Manassas Junction, and on August 27 the ragged and famished Confederates feasted on potted lobster, sausages, butter, champagne and all the other luxuries the Union had squirreled away for its boys. Then Old Jack set the supplies on fire.

Alarmed at the sight of distant smoke billowing up from his lost stores and learning that there was now an army, led by none other than Stonewall Jackson, between his troops and Washington, Pope was nearly beside himself. But after a detachment of Federals defeated (so Pope erroneously thought) some of Jackson's troops under Ewell at Broad Run (it was merely a strategic retreat), Union victory again

seemed sure. Pope imagined Jackson holed up in the trenches of Manassas Junction waiting for General Lee. So, advancing a huge force at dawn on the 28th, Pope lumbered towards Manassas Junction, only to find that Jackson had vanished.

How had Jackson evaded him? While Pope watched Manassas Junction go up in smoke, Stonewall had simply gone north under cover of night, bivouacked in the Groveton woods and then selected a strategic point for battle that made room for Lee to join them and, if need be, gave the Confederates an escape route. From there he could, alternatively, attack the enemy's flank while Lee attacked from another direction before Pope could be reinforced. Not far away was still another Confederae division under W. B. Taliaferro, augmented by troops under Ewell.

On the afternoon of the 28th Confederate cavalry captured a Federal courier with a message from McDowell for his left and center troops to move to Manassas Junction. Taliaferro described Stonewall's reaction when he received the message:

> The Captured dispatch roused Jackson [he and his men were sleeping] like an electric shock. He was essentially a man of action. He rarely, if ever, hesitated. He never asked advice. He called no council to discuss the situation disclosed by this communication, although his ranking officers were almost at this side. He asked no conference of opinion. He made no suggestion, but simply, without a word, except to repeat the language of the message, turned to me and said: "Move your division and attack the enemy;" and to Ewell, "Support the attack." The slumbering soldiers sprang from the earth at the first murmur.

Eight brigades – 8000 Rebel troops – converged near Groveton, a mere tumble of cottages at the bottom of a long hill. A Union force of 10,000 men under Rufus King would oppose them, but King would be handicapped by a lack of cavalry. Jackson assembled the Confederates a mile from the Warrenton highway (the main road) on a ridge overlooking open ground. The Federals marched blithely along, thinking their enemy still at Manassas.

In the battle that followed Ewell was killed on the first charge, and his brigade lost 725. Jackson's Brigade lost 200. The western Union brigade under John Gibbon lost 750 but remained unbeaten. Tactically, the engagement appeared

Above left: *So vital were the railroads for carrying men and supplies that they faced continual attack by both armies. This railroad bridge over Bull Run, near Manassas, Virginia, had been destroyed but was rebuilt by army road engineers.*

Left: *Virginia infantry at their camp in the woods near Leesburg, Virginia.*

Right: *The Second Battle of Bull Run, fought on August 29-30, 1862, marked the successful completion of a long Confederate campaign to save Richmond and free Virginia of Federal troops.*

Below: *Encampment protecting Warren railroad station at Warrenton, Virginia.*

to be a draw, but it had the effect of luring the whole Federal army onto Jackson. Pope made ready to attack in the morning, thinking to finish Stonewall off.

The Union forces were, however, in disarray and so spread out that they failed to get vital communications to headquarters. Thus Pope was totally unaware that Longstreet had sent Federals on either side of Throughfare Gap running or that another Federal division had abandoned Groveton field at 1:00AM. Jackson, too, lacked information; he did not know that Longstreet had broken through, and he was not counting on immediate support.

On the morning of August 29 18,000 Confederate infantrymen and 2500 cavalry encountered almost as many troops under Franz Sigel and John Reynolds not far from Bull Run Creek. The battle was fierce. One combattant described Jackson waiting for Longstreet's force in the heat of conflict: "I rode along with him, and all he said was: 'Two hours, men, only two hours; in two hours you will have help. You must stand it for two hours.'" Miraculously they did, and they cheered wildly when Longstreet arrived that noon.

After a lull the battle was resumed in the late afternoon. It raged inconclusively along a five-mile front, while casualties on both side soared, and only died down when General John Hood and his Texas Brigade drove back the Union's Philip Kearny, and broke the final Union advance. So ended the first day of the Second Battle of Bull Run (or Second Manassas).

Both Lee and Pope thought the other side would withdraw after such carnage. But the 30th saw both armies still in place, with Jackson commanding the Rebel left, and Longstreet the right. Attack and counterattack followed one another until the Union's Fitz-John Porter foolishly committed his infantry on the left and Pope refused to send him reinforcements. The resutant overwhelming of the Union line here marked the decisive moment. By the afternoon Longstreet's artillery was moving down Federals like summer grass, and then Lee unleashed the final massive attack. By sunset the battle had been won by the South, and, with Jackson's troops leading the pursuit, Pope was retreating in total defeat.

Above: *Confederate soldiers lie where they fell. After the first day's carnage at the Second Battle of Bull Run, each side expected the other to withdraw. The next day found both armies still in place.*

Below; *General Stonewall Jackson held off Pope on the second day at Bull Run until Longstreet arrived to catch the Federals in a pincers. Jackson's men led the pursuit of the fleeing Union troops.*

The Maryland Invasion

The Second Battle of Bull Run might have been a more decisive victory for the Confederates if their army had been able to press its advantage. As it was, on September 1 General Lee ordered Jackson to pursue Pope's defeated armies through a fierce thunderstorm that left much of both forces' ammunition wet. Jackson moved his forces up to Chantilly, a gutted mansion along the road to Fairfax, and a brief but fierce contest there cost the Confederates 800 casualties to the Union's 1300.

Half of Jackson's forces never even engaged the enemy at Chantilly because the weather literally put a damper on the battle. In fact, Jackson's own Brigade saw no action, although some of its members were later asked to help bury the numerous dead. Like the entire Second Manasses Campaign, Chantilly had been a costly encounter that fell short of being decisive. Nevertheless, the Richmond papers had a field day:

> Little Be-Pope, he came at a lope,
> Jackson, the Rebel, to find him.
> He found him at last, then ran very fast,
> With his gallant invaders behind him!

On September 2 the Federals were ordered back to Washington, for, given the proximity of Manassas to Washington, the Union was again fearful for its capital. And well they might be, for very shortly President Davis would be ordering Jackson to cross the Potomac and form the advance guard of an invasion of the North.

The plan to invade Maryland was Lee's, and it was motivated by several hopes. One was that a Confederate victory might win the hearts and minds of sympathizers in the border areas. Further, if Jackson or Lee could score a major Southern victory on enemy soil there was the hope that this might sway Northern voters in favor of pro-peace candidates and even entice Europe governments to recognize the sovereignty of the Confederacy. Finally, there was simply the hope that a victory in Maryland would produce a helpful degree of military, economic and political disruption and would further sap the North's will to fight.

On September 4 Jackson's command left the Manassas plains, heading toward the Potomac with the goal of crossing and continuing on to Frederick, Maryland. On Septem-

A call for Tennessee volunteers. Second only to Virginia as a battleground, Tennessee sent more soldiers to the Civil War – 145,000 – than any other Southern state.

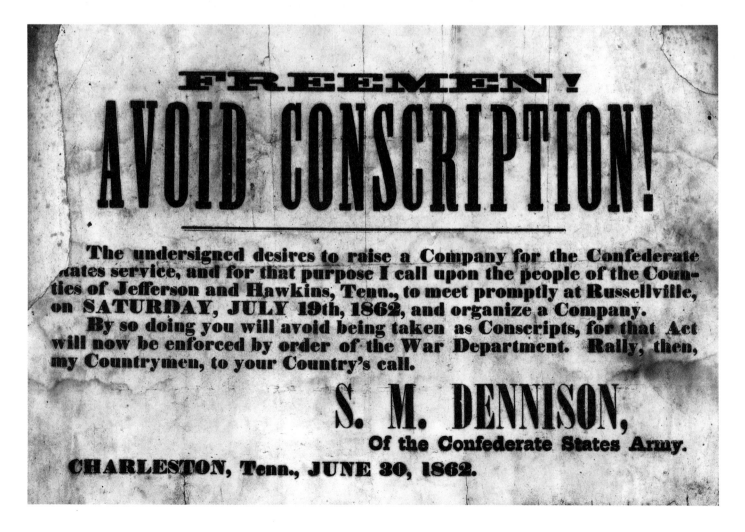

Left: *Union encampment with General McClellan's tent shown at center.*

Below: *A Company of Union troops drawn up on Maryland Heights at Harpers Ferry.*

Photograph of part of the battlefield at Antietam, Maryland, taken on the day of the battle.

ber 6 Jackson, close behind the Federals, who were heading toward Alexandria, reached White's Ford on the Potomac, crossed and occupied Frederick the next day. Supposedly, when he marched through Frederick, he passed by the house of Barbara Frietchie, an elderly woman who persisted in flying the Union flag. According to the poem by John Greenleaf Whittier, after Jackson ordered it shot down, she cried out:

"Shoot, if you must, this old gray head,
But spare your country's flag," she said.
Although it has never been proven that such an incident really occured, an old woman of this name did in fact live in Frederick.

Jackson's cavalry, under the indomitable Stuart, created a virtual wall of pickets that kept McClellan (who had now replaced the ineffectual Pope) from determining the Confederate position or even if all or just part of Lee's forces had crossed the Potomac. However, behind the Confederate forces lay Harper's Ferry, strongly garrisoned by Federals, a town which was at once a protection against invasion of the Shenandoah and beartrap for invaders of the North. Lee now decided to split off a large part of his force to take Harper's Ferry, and to this effect he issued his famous Special Order 191.

In essence the order divided the Confederate forces into two main commands. The Army's left wing was Jackson's

Currier & Ives print of the bloodiest single day of the war, the Battle of Antietam, September 17, 1862.

responsibility, while Lee took charge of the right. Having thus divided the Confederate forces, Lee took several divisions northwest to Hagerstown, and Jackson and his wing (some 25,000 men) left for Harper's Ferry at dawn on September 10. Jackson, under Lee's orders, marched in secret, feigning a Pennsylvania destination by asking the locals directions for roads leading there.

By September 13 Jackson's forces had surrounded the town. At this point the Union had a stroke of luck. Near Frederick, John Bloss, a Union soldier who had stopped to rest from a skirmish with the Rebels, found a copy of Lee's Special Order No. 191. "I noticed a large envelope. It was not sealed and when I picked it up two cigars and a paper fell out," he later recounted. Upon reading it, he realized that the paper contained Lee's secret orders to Jackson and contained a wealth of information about the Southern commanders' intentions and troop dispositions. This valuable paper was soon in the hands of McClellan.

How the orders got lost is still a mystery. Some suggest that Jackson never parted with his own copy and that what was found was an aide's. Whoever was to blame, the invasion of Maryland was now seriously compromised.

As Jackson headed for Harper's Ferry word of McClellan's find got back to Lee, whose army was still scattered and vulnerable. Lee desperately tried to delay McClellan – who was now moving towards Jackson with his usual lack of energy – by intercepting the Union General at South Mountain, using the nearest available troops (D. H. Hill's small division of 8000 men). On September 14, Hill engaged MClellan there and lost.

Jackson, in the meantime, had failed to trap the Federals at the Martinsburg Arsenal across the river in Virginia, and his intended prey hastily joined the garrison at Harper's Ferry. Early on the morning of September 15 Stonewall's Brigade assumed a position on a high bluff overlooking the strategic town, while the batteries of his artillerymen Poague and Carpenter hammered away at the Federal garrison from yet another elevation. Jackson then cut off all of his enemy's escape routes, and by 7:30 that morning, the Federals had raised a white flag of truce. Jackson had captured Harper's Ferry with artillery alone; no more than 100 of his men had been lost.

After a brief rest, at 2:00 in the morning of the 16th Jackson ordered the Brigade out on another of his early morning marches. His destination this time was to join the main Confederate force at Sharpsburg, Maryland. Before they set out, Jackson's men had already marched for three and a half days nearly nonstop and had covered more than 60 miles. They had crossed two mountain ranges, forded the Potomac twice, lain siege to Harper's Ferry and had just taken the town. Now they were on the road again. With troop movements accomplished in such a fashion, there were inevitable stragglers, soldiers too weary and hungry to keep up the pace. One woman along the route from Martinsburg recorded the words of a Rebel straggler who knocked on her door: "I been a-marchin' an' a-fightin' for six months stiddy, and I ain't had n-a-r-thin' to eat 'cept green apples an' green cawn, an' I wish you'd please gimme a bite to eat." On the march to Sharpsburg the straggling grew epidemic, with only 250 men – new volunteers included – arriving on time. Even hard-driving Stonewall, it was said, termed the march "severe."

The knowledge that the Federals had discovered his battle plans had forced Lee to abandon his offensive and

Harpers Ferry, Virginia, in 1861 after it was abandoned by Confederate soldiers trying to avoid being cut off by Union troops under Generals McClellan and Patterson, who were advancing from the north and west.

10:30 AM Jackson's outnumbered troops were driven back to the West Wood, on the far side of Hagerstown Pike. The Confederate left was now in grave danger, and the Federals were applying massive pressure on the center.

But somehow, at times by stripping his right, Lee was able to reinforce every threatened point with enough men to hold the Rebel line intact. On the left the remnants of

Left: *Union General Ambrose Burnside's division crossing the bridge at Antietam. In fact, the Union troops could have waded across the creek at this point.*

Below left: *The bridge at Antietam shortly after the battle. Today it bears Burnside's name.*

Below: *Fallen Confederate artillerymen on Antietam battlefield. The battle concluded with both sides exhausted and with enormous losses. Jackson's division alone had lost 700 of its 1800 men.*

address the problem of confronting McClellan's juggernaut. That confrontation is remembered in history as the Battle of Antietam Creek, or Sharpsburg, as the South called it.

Early on the 16th Jackson arrived at Sharpsburg with the first of his reinforcements. He found Lee already battling the Federals. Jackson's troops were few, depleted and tired; his other units, under A. P. Hill and Lafayette McLaws, had not yet arrived. The Confederates were already lined up along the west bank of Antietam Creek, and on the opposite bank, McClellan's forces were fully deployed, with Generals Joseph Hooker, Joseph Mansfield and Edwin Sumner to the right; General Fitz-John Porter in the center; and on the left, Ambrose Burnside.

By the 17th more of Jackson's troops from Harper's Ferry were coming up. Pickets had spent the night so close to one another that either side could hear each other's footsteps. Confederates and Federals were now lined up in a row three miles long. A mile north of the village, near Dunkard Church, Jackson assumed the left side of the Confederate position, one which unfortunately offered no cover except fence-rails and rocky ledges. By 5:00 in the morning the main battle had begun.

Confederate artillerymen lobbed canister at wave after wave of blue-coated infantry, and Jackson's men surprised attacking enemy soldiers by suddenly standing up and firing point blank into the first wave. From the nearby trees Poague's battery exchanged fire with Federal guns. At about

Jackson's division hung on grimly, taking cover behind a ledge of rocks and pounding away at the enemy. Finally, it was the Federal line opposite Jackson that wavered. The Confederates began to move forward, and the Yanks retreated, leaving 300 dead, with total casualties of 3000.

In another part of the field, because men had to be taken to help Jackson in the West Wood and around Dunkard Chapel, the Confederates' General Robert Toombs and his one brigade were left to hold off the Union's Burnside for three hours at Burnside's Bridge. Eventually they were driven back, and for a time it seemed that the Rebel line would be broken, but once again reinforcements arrived just in time, and the line re-formed. Although this was not Jackson's immediate arena, it was typical of the way that the battle progressed: so many men were lost, so many regiments and brigades were nearly obliterated, that trying to cover for one unit's losses by importing reinforcements from another part of the field became a nightmare. Confederate General Longstreet spoke with quaint accuracy of "this field of seldom-equalled strife."

Antietam, the bloodiest single day of this profoundly bloody war, ended in a draw. Kyd Douglas, voluble chronicler of the Stonewall Brigade's campaigns, described the evening of the 17th: "nearly all of them were wandering over the field, looking for their wounded comrades, and some . . . doubtless, plundering the dead bodies of the enemy left on the field. Half of Lee's army was hunting the other half." Brigade member Ned Moore described the two armies next day: "the two armies lay face to face, like two exhausted monsters, each waiting for the other to strike."

That next day, in fact, neither force seemed capable of movement, much less active combat. The South had lost 13,724 men killed or wounded, the North 12,410. Both sides were ready to disengage. As McClellan wrote, ". . . at this critical juncture – Virginia lost, Washington menaced, Maryland invaded – the national cause could afford no risks of defeat. One battle lost, and almost all would have been lost." For different but analogous reasons Lee, too, felt that he had had enough.

Jackson and Lee evacuated with amazing alacrity during the night of the 18th-19th, and this further discouraged pursuit by McClellan. Jackson's Brigade was in bad shape, as was his division: the 250-member Brigade had lost 88 wounded or dead, and the division had lost 700 of its 1800 men. Confederate wounded and dying filled the roads toward Winchester, the direction of the Confederate retreat. The invasion of the North was now no more than a memory.

Fredericksburg

Except for cavalry scouts, Jackson was the last Confederate soldier to cross the Potomac after Antietam. A little later, at dusk, a small number of Federal infantry corssed to attack two rear-guard Rebel brigades. Lee immediately sent a courier to give Jackson orders to quell the attack, but Stonewall had already heard the news and had sent Jubal Early and A. P. Hill to meet the enemy while he went ahead to assess the situation. The Federals were both outnumbered and quickly outflanked. Johnny Reb was still a potent foe.

From September 20 to November 22 Jackson camped near Winchester. Like the Federals, the Confederates were still reeling from the blows inflicted at Antietam, and desertion and indiscipline were rampant. Lee formed a guard to take in stragglers near Winchester and sent cavalry to protect farms from marauders. Meanwhile, Lee and Jackson pondered the lessons of the recent past. The lessons were grim enough. The Maryland invasion had accomplished little. They had overestimated McClellan's caution, and those who praticipated in the battle admitted that they had underestimated the skill and tenacity of the Federal soldier. And now the Confederate army itself was in disarray.

On October 2 Lee wrote to President Davis asking that the Army of Virginia be reorganized into two corps, with Longstreet at the head of one and Jackson in command of the other. On October 11 Jackson was officially promoted to Lieutenant-General and given command of the Second Army Corps. Under his command was his own division, A. P. Hill's (the Light) Division, Richard Ewell's division and D. H. Hill's division, together with Colonel Brown's battalion of artillery – 1917 officers, 25,000 soldiers and 126 guns. Stonewall bypassed Colonel Andrew Jackson Grigsby to assign Frank Paxton, a friend and fellow Presbyterian, as new commander of the Stonewall Brigade. Outraged, Grigsby retired to private life.

Jackson's reputation in the Confederacy had by this time risen very high. From being a much-ridiculed VMI professor, "Tom Fool," Jackson had become an adored hero of the South. His men cheered him wherever he went, so much so that whenever a loud yell came from Jackson's camps, men would say, "That's Jackson or a rabbit!" They hardly ever called him "Stonewall." He was mostly "Old Jack," "Old Blue Light" (an outsider's comment on his piety), "Hickory" or "Square Box" (a reference to his big feet). Jackson returned his troops' adoration with admiration of his own: "You cannot praise these men of my brigade too much; they

Left: *After the battle at Antietam, President Abraham Lincoln visited his generals at the battlefield. Lincoln used the appearance of Union victory as an opportunity to release his Emancipation Proclamation.*

Above: *Known for his piety, General Stonewall Jackson (standing, left) leads a prayer service in camp. The seated general on the left is A. P. Hill and standing at Jackson's left is General R. S. Ewell.*

Left: *A sketch of General Jackson made in December 1862 at a staff supper.*

Right: *Uniform of a soldier of the Confederate Maryland Guard.*

have fought, marched and endured more than I ever thought they would."

Jackson's slightest peculiarities became exalted: his habit of visibly praying in battle, his utter disregard for crisp military attire, his frequent blushing, his veneration of clergymen, his old-fashioned manners. "Stonewall died," his troops joked, "and two angels came down from heaven to take him back with them. They went to his tent. He was not there. They went to the hospital. He was not there. They went to the outposts. He was not there. They went to the prayer-meeting. He was not there. So they had to return without him; but when they reported that he had disappeared, they found that he had made a flank march and reached heaven before them."

As the weather turned cold Valley residents took up a collection for Old Jack and his men: one newspaper, Staunton's *Spectator and General Advertiser,* lists a contribution from Rockbridge County of 175 blankets, 75 pairs of socks, 50 pairs of shoes, leather for 50 more pair and $750 in cash. Picket duty now was the extent of military obligations for the ordinary soldier in Jackson's ranks; and the highlight of their stay in Winchester was a tent revival, of which one regiment's chaplain wrote, "Thirty-five soldiers have professed to be converted. Daily meetings are being held, and the numbers are manifesting a deep interest in reference to spiritual things." This "deep interest" seemed to rise dramatically whenever Old jack strode through camp, and he more than once led the entire brigade – more hastily assembled than he knew – in prayer.

Neither his men nor Jackson were able to rest on their laurels for long, for now McClellan, under pressure from Lincoln, was preparing for a winter campaign. He had been accused of procrastination after Antietam, though his inaction may have been justified by lack of essential supplies. But now there was also a political consideration. Five days after the Battle of Antietam, Lincoln had issued the Emancipation Proclamation. The Democratic party did not endorse it, and there was much controversy about it in the North, even within the Union army. A swift thrust into Virginia, reasoned Lincoln and his advisers, might help to mute factionalism in the ranks and encourage them with victory.

In October, 1862, Union Secretary of War Halleck wrote McClellan, "The President orders you to cross the Potomac and give battle to the enemy or drive him south. Your army must move now while the roads are good." McClellan complained bitterly. "Did they not know that a large part of our troops were in want of shoes, blankets, and other indispensible articles, notwithstanding all the efforts that had been made since the battle of Antietam, and even prior to that date, to refit the army?" Even General George Meade the future victor at Gettysburg, wrote to his wife of the perplexing sluggishness of the Union's response to McClellan's request for essential supplies.

The hardened "foot cavalry" of Stonewall Jackson had long since learned to put up with such inconveniences. Nor did they stand still while McClellan waited to restock with shoes, blankets, overcoats, ammunition and forage. Early in October, and for the second time in the conflict, Jackson's cavalry Colonel Jeb Stuart launched a series of raids right under McClellan's nose. Stuart made off with horses, took a few prominent prisoners to trade off for Confederate ones and spent, at one stretch, some 56 hours behind enemy lines about 30 miles from McClellan's headquarters.

On October 26, 1862, an exasperated McClellan crossed the Potomac into Virginia. But on November 7 he was summarily relieved of his leadership and replaced by an unwilling and self-declared bad choice, General Ambrose Burnside. At the same time, Jackson was negotiating with Lee to consider a proposed change in strategy. Rather have the two portions of the Confederate forces reunited, as Lee wanted to do, Jackson suggested that he be allowed to stay put behind the Blue Ridge. Such a position would give him maneuverability and the capacity to aim at the Union's flank and rear rather than having to face off with the Federals with inferior numbers. This was sound advice, but it was premature, since the confusion in Union command meant that many changes in Union movement would occur before troops engaged.

Burnside decided to move his army to Fredericksburg, Virginia, to cross the adjacent Rappahannock River and to take the heights south of Frederickburg. In mid-November Jackson had moved to Winchester, and the Union again feared for its capital; but on the 22nd he left Winchester and arrived on the 27th at the Orange Court House, 36 miles from Fredericksburg. Meantime, Lee also sent Longstreet to Fredericksburg.

Jackson placed his troops almost entirely in the woods. Nearby, on the other side of the river, the Federal troops assembled. The Bluecoats flashed their bayonets in the sun, and their regimental banners snapped bravely in the winds, but the crisis of leadership weighed upon the Federals', and their morale was low. There was almost unanimous opposition to Burnside's strategy by his officers, and the Union government, in its turn, delayed them by sluggish delivery of pontoons with which to cross the Rappahannock. When the pontoons finally did arrive Jackson's sharpshooters, "hornets that were stinging the Army of the Potomac into a frenzy," cut down soldier after soldier as they tried to effect their crossing.

The Confederates had had plenty of time to arrange themselves suitably. Longstreet off on the left, was ensconced on Marye's Heights, the best seat in the house, as it were. Jackson, on the right flank, occupied a hill near Hamilton's Crossing.

On December 13, after fits and starts during the two previous days, the Battle of Fredericksburg began in earnest. From the beginning, Jackson and the other Confederate troops had the battle in their hands. Federals repeatedly tried to charge Marye's Hill over an open field, only to be mowen down like grass. Their famed "Irish Brigade" under General Thomas Meagher lost all but 250 men that way. From Stafford Heights Union artillery poured fire down upon Jackson's Brigade and did some execution, but at no point was the issue of the battle ever in doubt.

When the fighting ended the appalling extent of the Union's humiliation was clear: it had lost 12,653, while the Confederates lost but 5309. Burnside, by this own request, was relieved on his command shortly after his disaster. Jackson had done his part at Fredericksburg, but there was little satisfaction for him or any of the other Confederate victors in that day's slaughter.

Below: *Federal troops cross the Rappahannock by scow and pontoon bridge on December 12, 1862, the day before their doomed assault on the Rebel forces at Fredericksburg.*

Above: *A Confederate artilleryman. Jackson's artillery at Fredericksburg did major damage to Union troops, tearing wide holes in their lines as they advanced on his position.*

Left: *Soldiers lie dead on Marye's Heights. Union soldiers threw themselves again and again at the Confederate position, but by the end of the day not one Federal soldier had reached the Southern lines.*

Above: *Repulse of Federal troops at Marye's Heights, where the Confederate army was well positioned.*

Below: *Wreckage of caisson wagons destroyed on Marye's Heights by a Union siege gun.*

Chancellorsville

After the battle at Fredericksburg, Lee and Jackson's troops gladly went into winter quarters at Moss's Neck on the Rappahannock. Old Jack's men had longed to go into winter quarters, as that meant no more shivering in flimsy canvas tents, but warmer, studier housing and a respite from all the privations that winter adds to active warfare. Called "Camp Winter" by the troops, recruits' quarters at Moss Neck were mostly erected from chopped trees, re-assembled as cabins by the soldiers over holes three to five feet deep. Some other soldiers constructed barricaded tents, reinforced with wood and augmented with a chimney and fireplace at one end. A few simply buried themselves deep in the snow or dirt for the night, in what they called "gopher holes."

Though finding food was a challenge, and malnutrition from poor diet was not unusual, one captain wrote to his wife, "As to eating, we still do very well; we have bread, none of your flat cakes but nice light rolls, beef rather poor but makes good hash, salt port, none of the best but makes good shortening and rye coffee well sugared." Apples were available, but the general absence of fruit and fresh vegetables left many, including the Stonewall Brigade's General Frank Paxton, ill for the duration of the winter.

Even in winter Jackson's habitual harshness did not soften. Wintering was, for Old Jack, the time for polishing up his troops. That meant discipline, which, in turn, meant punishment. And Jackson's idea of punishment was often extreme. Not only did he bring back flogging for ordinary failures of discipline but he continued to punish desertion with the firing squad. In February, 1863, when Jackson condemned three deserters from the Stonewall Brigade to death by firing squad, he wrote, "The Army Regulations define the duty of all who are in the service, and departure from its provisions lead to disorganization and deficiency." An unwilling Kyd Douglas was picked to be the executioner, but on the day of the execution a pardon arrived from Presi-dent Davis. Many suspected that it came at the instigation of Robert E. Lee.

One prisoner in Jackson's brig for a variety of minor offenses wrote: "I found two or three hundred in the guard house, and the court martial in full blast. Punishments of all kinds were being inflicted on the prisoners, such as shot to death, whipped, heads shaved and drummed out of service, riding wooden horses, wearing barrel shirts, and other punishments in the catalogue of court martials."

This was also a period when Jackson's contentiousness blossomed. He and A.P. Hill had been at odds since the Maryland campaign. In September of 1862 Hill had voiced his objections to Jackson's interfering with Hill's command of his troops in mid-battle. Jackson considered this insub-ordinate and answered, "Put up your sword and consider yourself under arrest." Even G. F. R. Henderson, one of Jackson's more rhapsodic biographers, admits that Jackson seldom ever forgave others' mistakes. He notes that Stone-wall had always resented Hill's tardiness at Cedar Run, and the incident in September undoubtedly added fuel to an already smoldering fire. Though Hill had fought hard and well in Fredericksburg, wintering seemed to exacerbate Jackson's ire, and it was at this time that Jackson chose to press Hill for "satisfaction." Some accounts suggest that a duel might have been the outcome (Jackson, it is reported, acted twice as a second in duels in Mexico) but none was actually fought. All through the spring of 1863 this conflict kept Lee busy trying to defuse the effects of recriminations and unanswered letters. The temperature plummeted

View of Fredericksburg across the Rappahannock in February 1863. Jackson was now in winter quarters, where he used the time to prepare for a speedy victory in the spring.

Confederate troops on the destroyed Fredericksburg Bridge. While in winter quarters Lee and Jackson planned their next campaigns.

whenever A. P. Hill and Stonewall met, and there was an agonizing stiffness between the two.

In November, 1862, Stonewall Jackson became the father of a baby girl. His wife later wrote notstalgically of Stonewall's pleasure then: "To a man of his extreme domesticity, and love for children, his was a crowning happiness; and yet, with his great modesty and shrinking from publicity, he requested that he should not receive the announcement by telegraph, and when it came to him by letter, he kept the glad tidings to himself – leaving his staff and those around him in the camp to hear of it from others." Jackson named his daughter Julia Laura, after his mother and his sister.

But Stonewall was not to see his daughter or his wife until April, 1863, though he evidently yearned for them. His chief of staff, the Presbyterian minister Reverend Major R. L. Dabney, proposed to Old Jack that Mrs. Jackson visit Dabney's home and that Stonewall join them. Jackson declined. "It is better for me to remain with my command so long as the war continues. . . . Whilst it would be a great comfort to me to see you and our darling little daughter, and others in whom I take a special interest, yet duty appears to require me to remain with my command." he wrote to his wife. Finally, Anna and the baby came, and the general moved to Hamilton's Crossing at the Yerby plantation.

Even then Jackson did not neglect his military duties, but spent most of his time at the post. His leisure, however, was devoted to his wife and baby: "His devotion to his child was remarked upon by all who beheld the happy pair together," wrote his wife, "for she soon learned to delight in his caresses as much as he loved to play with her." On April 29, 1863, just before the troops began their move to Chancellorsville, Jackson sent his wife and child to Richmond, and (as one biographer notes), without eating his breakfast, he went back to his martial duties.

In January of 1863, as Lee and Jackson planned their next moves in Moss Neck, Burnside had made one last attempt to save face with the Union brass. Launching a campaign derisively called the "Mud March," Burnside had his troops advance on the Rappahannock on January 20, 1863. The troops first were caught in a 30-hour downpour and then became stuck in the mud of the January thaw. It took hours

for them to get matériel – caissons, horses, wagons, artillery – out of the mud, and battle was out of the question. On the other side of the river, Jackson's men had erected signs, when they realized their enemy's distress: "Burnside stuck in the mud" and "Yanks, if you can't place your pontoons yourself, we will send you help." On the 24th the rains subsided, and the sodden Union troops crept back to their base in disgrace.

Meantime, the South continued to drill, prepare and plan.

Indeed, the South would put more personnel in the field in Spring, 1863, than it did in any other year of the war, and this would put such a strain on Southern stomachs and pockets that a speedy victory was more than ever imperative. Jackson, with his instinct for the Union's jugular vein, was obviously one of the South's best bets to accomplish this.

On January 25, 1863, the Union's Army of the Potomac got a new commander, General Joseph ("Fighting Joe") Hooker. Hooker was a Mexican War alumnus who had been

Left; *Pontoon bridges across the Rappanhannock River in the spring of 1863. Some 40,000 Union troops were drawn up here opposite the Confederate positions.*

Above: *A Confederate sharp-shooter takes aim.*

Below: *Rebel cavalry ride into line of battle.*

a formidable foe at Second Manassas, South Mountain and Antietam, and he now stood at the head of a force of 125,000 to 130,000 troops (compared to Lee's 62,000). All winter in Yankee quarters Hooker, too, had drilled his troops and worked to restore morale and battle readiness.

Forty thousand Union troops were already located opposite the Rebel forces at Fredricksburg, and another 80,000 situated themselves around the upper fords of the Rappahannock, expecting to attack the Confederate flank. On

Above: *Generals Robert E. Lee and Stonewall Jackson in council. On the night of May 1, 1863, working closely together, they decided that Hooker had to be flanked.*

Right: *Two sketches of the battle at Chancellorsville by artist A. R. Waud. Above, Union forces repelling an attack by Jackson. Below, Hooker's field headquarters.*

April 27 Hooker began moving troops towards Chancellorsville. It was not a place to dart in and out of because it was surrounded by a nearly inpenetrable woods dubbed The Wilderness, but it was regarded as a place where one could gather one's troops effectively. (Actually, "Chancellorsville" was a bit of a misnomer: neither a town nor a village, it consisted merely of a single, rather grand mansion in a clearing.) According to Union General Regis de Trobriand, who analyzed Hooker's strategy after the war, when Hooker moved into Chancelorsville he neglected utterly to take into account that he would be up against the wily, fast-moving Stonewall. The Union commander simply thought that from where he was situated "he could strike the enemy, or at least force him to come out of his position, which was as weak from the rear as it was strong from the front."

On May 1 Jackson and Lee, as usual, divided their armies and then proceeded to attack Hooker's advancing force. Somehow Hooker was led to believe that the Rebels were being heavily reinforced. He hesitated, and the conflict ended in a draw. That night and the following day Jackson, with characteristic daring and the aid of a guide, performed the incredible feat of marching some 26,000 troops 16 miles through the tangled Wilderness, virtually under the Federal's noses but completely undetected, so as to be in position to attack Hooker's right flank.

The attack was delivered in the late afternoon of May 2, and it was devastating. Hooker's right wing collapsed, and only the intervention of Union artillery and the failing light prevented Jackson's men from rolling up the whole Federal line. It was the beginning of a Union disaster. That evening

Jackson and some of his other officers rode far ahead of the battle line, looking for enemy outposts so as to determine the position of the enemy's main body for the next day's encounter. Shots rang out from the Confederate lines, and shouts followed, "Cease firing. You are firing into your own men!" Jackson's Little Sorrel bolted from the clutch of men, but the general reined in his horse with what was now his one good hand. It was A. P. Hill, ironically, who helped take Jackson from his horse, inquiring of his wounds, which Jackson described as "very painful . . . the arm is broken."

Jackson was taken on a litter through artillery fire to Guiney's Station. His left arm had been shattered and had to be amputated just below the shoulder. While Jackson lay in the hospital Hooker's fortunes continued to unravel. Outflanked again and again, he was by May 4 in full retreat back across the Potomac. On May 7 the Stonewall Brigade retired to Hamilton's Crossing for rest and recuperation, but anxiety about the wounded Jackson hung over the men like a dark cloud. Then, on May 10, the news ricocheted down the lines – sudden, sharp, painful as any wound: Jackson was dead.

Left above: *Badly wounded at Chancellorsville, Jackson would die of pneumonia on May 10.*

Left below: *On the day of his death Jackson led his men to a brilliant victory.*

Below: *Map of the Battle of Chancellorsville, showing General Hooker's march up the Rappahannock from Fredericksburg, General Jackson's flanking maneuver, the engagement in the Wilderness and the Union retreat.*

Throughout the battle Hooker had never been able to bring more than a portion of his force to bear upon the swift-moving Confederates, and some speculated that Hooker was either temporarily stunned by a shell that blew up nearby or drunk. Hooker later commented to an enquiring general, "Doubleday, I was not hurt by a shell, and I was not drunk. For once I lost confidence in Hooker, and that is all there is to it." But the Union had lost only a battle; the Confederacy had lost their most brilliant general, their hero and possibly the only man who could have turned the tide for the South.

Anna and his family grieved, the whole Confederacy grieved and even many in the North were saddened by the demise of this gallant enemy. Lincoln himself alluded to the noble foe who had been lost. Lee was devastated. Shortly after Jackson was wounded Lee had written to a friend, "He (Jackson) has lost his left arm, but I have lost my right arm." On May 10 Lee had lost the whole man.

Drawn through the streets in a white-plumed hearse by white horses, Thomas Johnathan Jackson was lain in state at the Governor's mansion in Richmond, and mourners poured into the Confederate capital from all over the South. Funeral services were held in the Presbyterian Church at Lexington where Jackson had worshipped in more peaceful days. He was buried next to Ellie and their daughter.

On May 30, 1863, the Confederate War Department honored a request that the Stonewall Brigade be the only unit in the Rebel army with its own permanent name. (The custom was simply to designate brigades by the name of whoever happened to be commanding them at the time.) The Brigade stayed together – minus the awful casualties of succeeding battles – until the surrender at Appomatox.

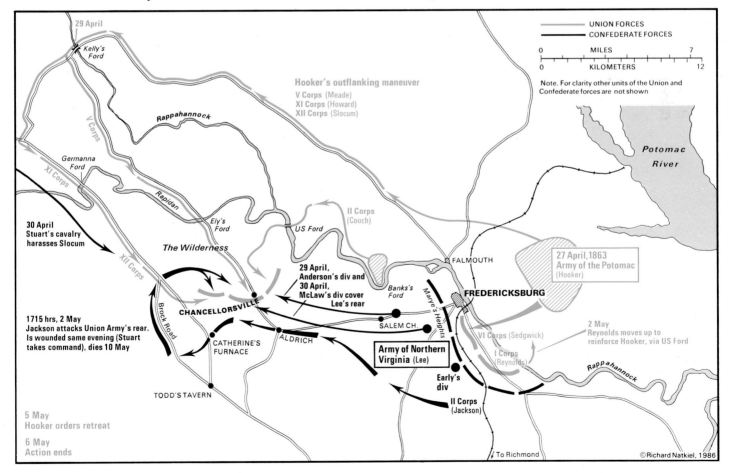

Man and Myth

The myth of Stonewall Jackson, which had already begun to burgeon in his lifetime, rapidly swelled to immense porportions after his death. Not only did the myth-makers credit him with military powers bordering on the supernatural, they simplified and adulterated his complex, not always attractive personality in ways that permitted him to fit more easily into the heroic role in which they were determined to cast him. The result has certainly been a disservice to historical understanding and probably even to Jackson's memory, since the mythic icon has always lacked

the humanity necessary to make it really credible. Yet disentangling the man from the myth is still by no means easy, and it is almost as hard to assess the full strategic significance of his military exploits.

In a sense, Stonewall Jackson was a very old-fashioned man. He died in defense of a way of life that flattered itself that it was similar to Athenian Greece but which, like Athens, depended upon the labor of human chattel to keep up its standard of living. Jackson no doubt truly believed that the Africans transported here were murderous at heart

and would be dangerous if not under the guidance of European-American masters, but he does not seem ever to have considered the matter more deeply. He also believed in the idea that the Federal government should stay out of the states' internal business, though he might have been hard put to define that business. For all his Southern independence, Old Jack found his best refuge in highly rigid structures: the army rules and regulations and the dogmas of a Calvinist Presbyterianism tinged with evangelism. Certainly he was eccentric – a hypochondriac, a man given to waving his arms in the air for no apparent reason, a soldier who refused to fight on Sundays. But, again, we cannot know if these were mere crotchets or symptoms of something more serious. A poor relation in an influential but roughshod family, Stonewall was an outsider to the nobility of the antebellum South, yet probably one of the reasons he became a Southern hero was because the common man of the South could identify with him.

Left: *A turn-of-the-century rendering of Stonewall Jackson at the Battle of Bull Run.*

Below: *Former comrades in arms gathered at the spot where Jackson fell.*

Right: *Jackson's second wife Anna did not see her husband between the birth of their daughter in November 1862 and April 1863, but she was at his side as he lay dying in May, and as she grieved, so did the Confederacy.*

Right: *A stone monument marks the spot where General Jackson fell. Richmond held a state funeral for him and he was buried in Lexington, Virginia, next to Ellie. Even the Federals mourned this loss of a great American.*

Below: *After Jackson's death his Stonewall Brigade went on to win many more battle honors. One of its fiercest fights was at Spotsylvania in May, 1864. In this last big Rebel victory the brigade suffered huge casualties.*

Basic to his character was the conflict between his passion for prayer and his passion for war. When asked by one of his students – who could not help but notice how "Tom Fool," the professor, suddenly became enthralled in drill – if he liked to fight, it is said that Stonewall got a strange look on his face. "Yes, I love to fight, but . . . I am principled against it."

A few biographers have been content to dismiss Jackson as an uncouth bumpkin from the West Virginia backwater, but the majority, like by Anna Jackson, his widow, have preferred to think of him as very close to the Almighty. (Anna staunchly defended his reputation against allegations of eccentricity or, for that matter, fallibility.) Some who knew him were not content with such simplicities. Seeing Jackson pray before the defense of Richmond, General Francis Taylor, for example, wrote:

Observing him closely, I caught a glimpse of the man's inner nature. It was but a glimpse. The curtain closed, and he was absorbed in prayer. Yet in that moment I saw an ambition. I saw an ambition as boundless as Cromwell's and as merciless.

No doubt the truth about the man eludes us still, but about his military genius there is general agreement. Yet even that has been subject to exaggeration. One priest who was attached to Paylor's Louisiana brigade began his prayerful dedication of a statue erected in Stonewall's honor with an address to the Almighty: "When in Thine inscrutable decree it was ordained that the Confederacy should fail, it became necessary for Thee to remove Thy servant Stonewall Jackson . . ." The notion that Jackson, had he lived, could have saved the South may be attractive to Southern hagiographers, but it is difficult to prove. One obvious difficulty is that up until the time of his death Jackson never had to confront a Union commander who could be rated better than a mediocrity. At least some of them had the grace not to make excuses. After Chancellorsville, Union General O. O. Howard, commander of the right wing which Jackson demolished, wrote:

Stonewall Jackson was able to mass a large force a few miles off . . . . There is always some theory which will forestall giving the credit of one's defeat to one's enemy. But in our own hearts, as we take a candid view of everything that took place in the Wilderness around Chancellorsville, we impute our defeat to the successful efforts of Stonewall Jackson and Robert E. Lee.

But suppose Jackson could have gone on to fight at Gettysburg. Could he have won? And if he had, would it have made a great difference, given Grant's simultaneous victory at Vicksburg? And how would Jackson have fared against Grant himself, a far more skilled officer than Lee had ever had to contend with before, after he was chosen to head up the Union army? We cannot know, and we should be far better off confining ourselves to the very great things that Jackson did accomplish than speculating about things he did not.

Jackson's tactics have often been compared to those of Napoleon, and indeed there is much similarity, though there is not much evidence of conscious emulation. Like Napoleon, he strove for as intimate a knowledge of the topography of a battle as possible (and when his cartographer, Jed Hotchkiss, failed him during the Peninsula campaign, Jackson's battles lost their focus) Such information facilitated his most Napoleon-like tactic, the surprise attack, in which Stonewall excelled.

Shortly after Stonewall died, his brilliant cavalry officer, Jeb Stuart, fell on May 13. Stuart, who cut a romantic figure and wrote a dashing chapter in the War Between the States,

Left: *Confederate notes and memorial poetry, including a $500 note with Stonewall Jackson's portrait.*

Overleaf: *Three Confederate soldiers pause on a march.*

Top: *General Joseph Hooker leading his Federal troops at the battle of Antietam.*

Above: *General Robert E. Lee with Generals Evans and Gordon at Spotsylvania. The question still remains: What if Jackson had been there?*

Right: *Lieutenant General Stonewall Jackson posed for this photograph two weeks before his death at Chancellorsville. The loss of this great tactician was not one the Confederacy could afford, and it marked a significant turning point in the Eastern theater of the war.*

was representative of another aspect of Jackson's tactical method. Old Jack's cavalry officers, Turner Ashby (who was killed before Jackson, at Harrisonburg on June 6, 1862) and Jeb Stuart were his scouts and his gadflies; and they successfully spied out and raided Union troop after Union troop in Jackson's most successful campaigns. Similarly, John Harmon, Jackson's profane and efficient Quartermaster, drove mules, slave labor and personnel and moved matériel for Stonewall with Draconian efficiency.

Another thing that made Jackson's military efforts so successful was his extensive use of spies. Belle Boyd, mentioned earlier, was a personal acquaintance. Jackson also made a point of ferreting out and questioning the best-informed local people he could find, and that lent substantially to Old Jack's ability to keep several jumps ahead of the enemy at all times. He used this tactic right to the end, when he sought the guidance of a certain foundry owner by the name of Wellford to help his men circle around the main body of Hooker's army. Hooker thought the woods were thick enough to protect him, but one Confederate prisoner jeered, "You may think you've done a great thing now, but wait till Old Jack gets around on your right."

With the death of the man, the tales of wonder about this leader who outfoxed the Yanks, grew into the myth of the great General of the Lost Cause. It is easy enough to discount the myth, but it is harder to turn our backs forever on those probably idle but inevitably fascinating questions: "What if he had lived? What if . . . ?"

Index